german
vocabulary
lisa kahlen
series editor
rosi mcnab

For over 60 years, more than
50 million people have learnt over
750 subjects the **teach yourself**
way, with impressive results.

be where you want to be
with **teach yourself**

For UK order enquiries: please contact Bookpoint Ltd, 130 Milton Park, Abingdon, Oxon, OX14 4SB. Telephone: +44 (0) 1235 827720. Fax: +44 (0) 1235 400454. Lines are open 09.00–17.00, Monday to Saturday, with a 24-hour message answering service. Details about our titles and how to order are available at www.teachyourself.co.uk

For USA order enquiries: please contact McGraw-Hill Customer Services, PO Box 545, Blacklick, OH 43004-0545, USA. Telephone: 1-800-722-4726. Fax: 1-614-755-5645.

For Canada order enquiries: please contact McGraw-Hill Ryerson Ltd, 300 Water St, Whitby, Ontario, L1N 9B6, Canada. Telephone: 905 430 5000. Fax: 905 430 5020.

Long renowned as the authoritative source for self-guided learning – with more than 50 million copies sold worldwide – the **teach yourself** series includes over 500 titles in the fields of languages, crafts, hobbies, business, computing and education.

British Library Cataloguing in Publication Data: a catalogue record for this title is available from the British Library.

Library of Congress Catalog Card Number: on file.

First published in UK 2003 by Hodder Education, 338 Euston Road, London, NW1 3BH.

First published in US 2003 by The McGraw-Hill Companies, Inc.

This edition published 2003.

The **teach yourself** name is a registered trade mark of Hodder Headline.

Copyright © 2003 Lisa Kahlen

In UK: All rights reserved. Apart from any permitted use under UK copyright law, no part of this publication may be reproduced or transmitted in any form or by any means, electronic or mechanical, including photocopy, recording, or any information, storage and retrieval system, without permission in writing from the publisher or under licence from the Copyright Licensing Agency Limited. Further details of such licences (for reprographic reproduction) may be obtained from the Copyright Licensing Agency Limited, of 90 Tottenham Court Road, London, W1T 4LP.

In US: All rights reserved. Except as permitted under the United States Copyright Act of 1976, no part of this book may be reproduced or distributed in any form or by any means, or stored in a database or retrieval system, without the prior written permission of the publisher.

Typeset by Transet Limited, Coventry, England.
Printed in Great Britain for Hodder Education, a division of Hodder Headline, 338 Euston Road, London, NW1 3BH, by Cox & Wyman Ltd, Reading, Berkshire.

The publisher has used its best endeavours to ensure that the URLs for external websites referred to in this book are correct and active at the time of going to press. However, the publisher and the author have no responsibility for the websites and can make no guarantee that a site will remain live or that the content will remain relevant, decent or appropriate.

Hodder Headline's policy is to use papers that are natural, renewable and recyclable products and made from wood grown in sustainable forests. The logging and manufacturing processes are expected to conform to the environmental regulations of the country of origin.

Impression number   10 9 8 7 6
Year   2008 2007 2006

Contents

There have been many studies carried out into the way we learn vocabulary. The Swiss, who are generally acknowledged as experts in multi-language learning, are also leaders in the understanding of the processes of language acquisition and some of their findings may be of interest to people wanting to broaden their vocabulary.

> Studies have shown that the most successful way [of learning vocabulary] is when the student is able to relate the new word to a concept and to integrate it into a conceptual system.
>
> (Wokusch, 1997)

Put simply this means that the most successful way of learning vocabulary is to put the new language into a context.

When a child first learns a language they are learning the concepts as well as the language at the same time. If you give a child an ice cream and say 'ice cream' they are learning the word and the concept at the same time, associating the word and the object. An adult has the advantage of already having the concept. An ice cream already conjures up other words: cold, vanilla, strawberry, like, don't like, size, price, etc.

Similarly if you decide to learn about a computer or a car you probably already know the parts or expressions you want to learn and can visualize them before you meet the word. In fact you already have the 'concept' and you can 'place' the new words within that concept.

It is for this reason that the vocabulary in this book has been given in context rather than, as in a dictionary, in alphabetical order. The words have been chosen as the words most likely to be useful or of interest to the learner.

One of the most useful tips in learning a new language is to look for ways of remembering a word: find a 'hook' to hang your new word or phrase on. We will now give you tips on how to make learning German words easier and more interesting.

How this book works

This book is more than just a list of words – it is a key to opening the door to better communication. It is designed to give you the confidence you need to communicate better in German by increasing your knowledge of up-to-date vocabulary and at the same time showing you how to use the new words you are learning.

The first part of the book includes some useful learning tips, rules on pronunciation and shortcuts to look out for when learning new words. The toolbox provides you with the tools you need to speak a language. It includes basic information about the structure of the language and useful tips, including how to address people, how to ask questions, how to talk about what you have done and what you are going to do, useful expressions and shortcuts to language learning. This part of the book is designed to be used for general reference.

The main part of the book is divided into topic areas: personal matters, family, work, education etc. Most adults complain that they find it very difficult to learn vocabulary and wish they had learnt it when they were younger. What they don't realize is that they are still trying to learn vocabulary in the same way as they did when they were children. The way the language is organized within the topic areas in this book is a direct result of studies carried out into language learning which show that adults find it difficult to learn long lists of words and find it easier to remember words if they are put into a context. The words have been carefully arranged, grouped with other related words, nouns, verbs, adjectives etc. and useful expressions with up-to-date notes about language fashions where relevant, so that the new language can be used immediately.

Make learning a list of words more interesting

- First decide which list you are going to look at today.
- See how many words you know already and tick them off.
- Choose which new words you want to learn – don't try to do too many at once but learn a certain amount each day.
- Count them so you know how many you are going to try to learn.
- Say them out loud; you could even record yourself saying them.

Remembering new words

- Try to associate the new words with words that sound similar in English: **Haus** (*house*).
- Try to associate the words with pictures or situations, e.g. try to imagine a picture of a rose when you say the word: **rosa**.
- Learn words in a context. Build a sentence with each new word you learnt.
- See if you can split the word into bits, some of which you know already: **Sommerferien = Sommer** (*summer*) + **Ferien** (*holidays*) = *summer holidays*; **Kinderlichtbildbescheinigung = Kinder** (*children*), **Lichtbild** (*photograph*), **Bescheinigung** (*certificate*) = *children's passport*.
- Look for words related to ones you know already: **Tag** (*day*), **täglich** (*daily*); **die Tageszeitung** (*daily paper*), **tagsüber** (*during the day*); **Sonne** (*the sun*), **sonnig** (*sunny*), **der Sonnenuntergang** (*sunset*), **Sonnenaufgang** (*sunrise*), **Sonntag** (*Sunday*).
- Look for words related to the English: **schwimmen** (*to swim*), **Vater** (*father*), **Storch** (*stork*).
- Look out for words which are the same in English and in German, but are pronounced differently: **die Inflation, die Imagination, die Butter, England**.
- Learn the value of typical beginnings and endings used to alter the meaning of words, e.g. **un; in; ehrlich/unehrlich** (*honest/dishonest*); **abhängig/unabhängig** (*dependent/independent*); **möglich/unmöglich** (*possible/impossible*).

Spelling tips

These don't always work but they may help!

- If a word begins with *th* in English, this often appears as a **d** in German: *Thursday*, **Donnerstag**; *to think*, **denken**; *thirsty*, **durstig**; *thanks*, **danke**.
- If a word begins with *p* in English, it is often **pf** in German: *pan*, **Pfanne**; *pipe*, **Pfeife**; *plaster*, **Pflaster**; *to pick*, **pflücken**.
- Where you see a word with the letter *k* in the middle, try replacing this with **ch**: *make*, **machen**; *cake*, **Kuchen**; *cook*, **kochen**; *weekly*, **wöchentlich**.
- Look out for words beginning with **im-, in-, re-, sub-** or **dis-** in German and begin the same in English. Words beginning with **des-** in German begin with *dis-* in English: **Immunität**, *immunity*; **inadäquat**, *inadequate*; **immateriell**, *immaterial*; **interessant**, *interesting*; **inflexibel**, *inflexible*; **Inflation**, *inflation*; **realistisch**, *real*; **reagieren**, *to react*; **reduzieren**, *to reduce*; **Substanz**, *substance*; **subventionieren**, *to subsidize*; **Diskothek**, *discotheque*; **disharmonieren**, *to be discordant*; **diskret**, *discreet*; **Desinfektion**, *disinfection*; **Desaster**, *disaster*.
- Many words which end in *-able* in English end in **-abel** in German: *acceptable*, **akzeptabel**; *comfortable*, **komfortabel**; *miserable*, **miserabel**.
- German ending **-ig** cognates with *-y* in English: *thirsty*, **durstig**; *hungry*, **hungrig**; *gawky*, **spindlig**.
- German ending **-sieren** cognates with *-ize* in English: **kritisieren**, *criticize*; **fantasieren**, *fantasize*; **modernisieren**, *modernize*.

Write words down

- Copy a list of the most important words onto A4 paper with a broad felt tip and stick it on the wall so that you can study it when doing some household jobs such as washing up, ironing, shaving or putting on make-up.
- For names of objects around the house, you could write the word on a sticky label and attach it to the actual object.
- Copy lists of words in German and English in two columns. First, say each word out loud, then cover up one column and try to remember each word in the other column.

- Do something else for half an hour and then come back and see how many you can still remember.
- Write down the first letter of each new word and put a dot for each missing letter, cover up the word and see if you can complete the word.
- Pick a few words you find difficult to remember: write each one down with the letters jumbled up; leave them for a while, then later try to unscramble each one.
- In your list, mark the difficult words: ask someone else to test you on the ones you have marked.

Shortcuts: looking for patterns

Certain letter patterns reveal important facts about the type of word you are trying to learn:

- Most nouns in German ending in -o, -tum, -ment, -eum, -ium, -um and -ett are neuter: **das Auto, das Radio, das Inferno, das Altertum, das Instrument, das Museum, das Delirium, das Duett.**
- Nouns in German ending in -age, -e, -ei, -heit, -keit, -schaft, -ie, -in, -ion, -tät, -ung are feminine: **die Garage, die Rose, die Malerei, die Frechheit, die Einsamkeit, die Eigenschaft, die Energie, die Medizin, die Infektion, die Universität, die Unterhaltung.**
- Most nouns in German ending in -el, -en, -er, -ig, -ich and -ling are masculine: **der Opel, der Wagen, der Teller, der Honig, der Kranich, der Feigling.**

You saw earlier in the introduction how other endings can convert one word into another; if you know the basic word, it is easy to work out the converted word. Similarly, some German words can be converted by adding a syllable at the beginning, and most work the same as in English, as follows:

ent-	= -de-/dis-	**entmachten** (*deprive*); **entdecken** (*discover*); **enträtseln** (*to decipher*)
ent-	= un-	**entladen** (*unload*); **entfalten** (*to unfold*)

The following syllables added to the beginning of a word can cause it to have the opposite or negative meaning:

un-	= un-	**freundlich** (*friendly*), **unfreundlich** (*unfriendly*); **angenehm** (*pleasant*), **unangenehm** (*unpleasant*)

miss- = *mis-/dis-*	verstehen (*to understand*), missverstehen (*misunderstand*); das Missgeschick (*misfortune*); Missachtung (*disregard*); missbilligen (*to disapprove*)
ver- = *for-*	bieten (*to offer*), verbieten (*forbid*); geben (*to give*), vergeben (*to forgive*)
in- = *in-*	tolerant, intolerant; diskret (*discreet*), indiskret (*indiscreet*), Insolvenz (*insolvency*)
des- = *dis-*	informiert (*informed*), desinformiert (*disinformed*); Solvenz (*solvency*)

Pronunciation

The alphabet

a	*ah*	j	*yot*	r	*err*
b	*beh*	k	*kah*	s	*ess*
c	*tseh*	l	*ell*	t	*teh*
d	*deh*	m	*em*	u	*oo*
e	*eh*	n	*en*	v	*fow*
f	*eff*	o	*oh*	w	*veh*
g	*geh*	p	*peh*	x	*iks*
h	*hah*	p	*peh*	y	*ueppsilon*
i	*ee*	q	*kuh*	z	*tsett*

If you wish to speak German with a good accent, the following tips will be useful; however it is always easier to listen to the pronunciation of a native German speaker.

1 German vowels are pronounced long or short depending on the consonants that follow. They are pronounced short if they are followed by two or more consonants, e.g. **alt, Geld**. They are pronounced long if they are followed by one consonant or by **h** and one consonant, **Tag, Bus, Jahr**.

---

a: long: **mag, Tag**; short: **Mann, wann**
e: long: **geht**; short: **Bett**
i: long: **ihn, ihm**; short: **Kind, bist**
o: long: **Dom**; short: **Obst**
u: long: **du, tun**; short: **Hund, und**

Note: the letter **e** is always pronounced at the end of the word, e.g. **Name, Schule, ich gehe**.

The vowels **a**, **o**, **u** sound different when they have dots (called *Umlauts*) over them: **ä**, **ö**, **ü**. They are best practised within a word. You might have heard them in names like **Müller**, **Jörg** and the word **Mädchen**.

2 Consonants: Most consonants are easy to pronounce for English learners.

The consonants **b**, **d**, **g** are pronounced the same in English at the beginning of the word: *bed*, **Bett**, *blue*, **blau**; *date*, **Datum**, *go*, **gehen**.

Note: The consonants **t**, **k** and **p** must be pronounced at the end of the word: **nicht**, **kaputt**, **krank**, **schlank**, **schlapp**. At the end of a word **b** is pronounced **p**: **Kalb**; and **d** prounounced **t**: **Hand**, **Wand**.

c is not often used on its own apart from in foreign words: **Café**, **Camping**. More often found in combination: **ch** sounds like **ck**: **Chaos**, **Charakter**

ch after **a**, **au**, **o** and **u** is pronounced like the Scottish word *loch*: **Dach**, **Bach**, **Strauch**, **Loch**, **doch**, **Buch**, **suchen**. After **e**, **ei**, **eu**, **i**, **ä**, **äu**, **ü**, **ch** sounds softer. **Teich**, **euch**, **ich**, **euch**, **Dächer**, **Bräuche**

g is the same as in English when preceding a vowel: **Wege**, **sagen**, when it is at the end of a syllable **g** is pronounced like a **k**: **weggehen**

h: you don't pronounce the **h** after a vowel, it just shows you that the vowel is pronounced long: **gehen**, **fehlen**, **Sohn**, **wohnen**, **Sahne**

j at the beginning of a word is pronounced as **y** in English: **Jugend**, **jodeln**

k: pronounce the **k** at the beginning and the end of a word: **krank**, **Kneipe**

l: the pronunciation is much lighter than English **l**

r before a vowel is pronounced by gargling slightly or spoken gutturally: **Rad fahren**, **regnen**. With another consonant or a single **r** at the end of the word (**lieber**, **wieder**) it is, however, much weaker and is pronounced like the **r** in English *here*

s is pronounced in two different ways: as in English *house*, before consonants and at the ends of words: **das**, **Haus**; as in English *busy*, when it precedes a vowel: **Rose**, **Saft**.

sch is pronounced like English *sh* in *sheep*: **schön**, **Fisch**

th: in German this is pronounced **t**: **Theorie**, **Theologie**

v sounds like English *for*, *from*

w sounds like English **v** *very*

ss, **ß** are pronounced **s**, **ss**

Two vowels together: **au** is pronounced **ow** in English *how* or *house*: **Aufzug**, **Tauben**, **Frau**.

Äu and **eu** as in English *boy*: **Mäuse**, **Gebäude**, **Freude**, **Eule**.

Ei sounds like English *eye*: **frei**, **drei**, **mein**.

Ie sounds like English *ee*: **Brief**, **Liebe**, **Bier**.

3 German intonation: the voice rises towards a comma and towards the end of a question but falls towards the end of a statement.

To sum up, once you are familiar with all these rules, German spelling and pronunciation are very reliable. (See pages 46–7 for more on German spelling.) Of course you won't learn them overnight, and it may be best to concentrate on learning and practising one at a time. Another useful method is to record and listen to spoken German as often as possible. Here are some ideas as to how you can make recordings of natural spoken German:

- Take a portable cassette player and some blank cassettes every time you go to Germany. Try recording from the local radio, or even people speaking, though you ought to ask their permission first!
- In some parts of the UK, especially in the south, you can sometimes pick up German radio: try playing around with your tuner, and if you find a German radio station, try to record some German.
- If you have German friends, ask them to make recordings for you, perhaps sending you messages with their family news, or giving their views on topics of interest to you.

- If you have satellite TV, see if you can also receive German television, and if not, talk to your local TV shop to ask if it is worth re-tuning your satellite equipment.
- If you have access to the internet, try to find German radio broadcasts via radio station websites.
- Once you have some recordings, listen to them as often as possible, and try to repeat what you hear, imitating the sounds and repeating short chunks of German. You might try writing out small sections, saying them out loud and comparing your version with the original.
- If you have German friends, try recording short messages on cassette; then send them to your friends, and ask them to comment on and correct your pronunciation.
- When speaking to German people, ask them to correct your pronunciation when possible.

toolbox

Nouns – gender and plurals

German nouns are very easy to spot: they always begin with a capital letter. Nouns are either masculine (m), feminine (f) or neuter(n). This is called the gender of a noun.

	m	f	n
Singular	der	die	das
Plural	die	die	die

There is often no logic as to whether a noun is masculine, feminine or neuter, so it's best to learn a new word plus its gender: don't just learn **Termin**, learn **der Termin**.

Tips on recognizing gender

You can recognize a feminine gender in most nationalities and occupations by the ending **-in**:

Engländer (m)	Engländerin (f)
Schotte (m)	Schottin (f)
Makler (m)	Maklerin (f)
Busfahrer (m)	Busfahrerin (f)

There are a few exceptions:
Deutsche (f)
Angestellte (f)

Masculine nouns (der): all days, months, and seasons are masculine:

der Montag	der Dienstag
der Januar	der Februar
der Frühling	der Sommer

All names for cars and long-distance trains are masculine:
    der BMW, der Mercedes, der VW
    der IC, der Euro-City, der InterCity Express

All names for lakes are masculine (as the word for lake *der* See):
    der Tegernsee
    der Bodensee
    der Wannsee

Usually, names of alcoholic drinks are masculine:
    der Vodka, der Schnaps, der Wein (exception: *das* Bier)

Neuter nouns (das): names of hotels, cafés and theatres: das Hotel zum Hang, das Hotel Kranz, das Hilton Hotel. Names of colours: das Rot, das Gelb. Most metals: das Kupfer, das Aluminium.

Most tree names are feminine: die Fichte, die Tanne, die Buche, but: *der* Ahorn.

Most flowers and fruits are feminine: die Osterglocke, die Nelke, die Rose, die Kirsche, die Banane, die Zitrone, but: *der* Apfel.

Nouns which end in **-age, -e, -ei, -heit, -keit, -schaft, -ie, -in, -ion, -tät** or **-ung** are almost always feminine: die Garage, die Tankstelle, die Malerei, die Frechheit, die Einsamkeit, die Eigenschaft, die Energie, die Medizin, die Infektion, die Universität, die Schaltung.

Nouns which end in **-el, -en, -er, -ig, -ich** or **-ling** are usually masculine: der Apfel, der Magen, der Gärtner, der Honig, der Kranich, der Feigling.

Nouns which end in **-tum, -ment, -eum, -ium, -um** or **-ett** are usually neuter: das Altertum, das Instrument, das Museum, das Delirium, das Duett.

Remember: the last word of a compound word determines the gender.
    der Ferienort
    die Ferien + **der** Ort = **der** Ferienort
    die Autobahn
    das Auto + **die** Bahn = **die** Autobahn

Plural

ℹ Every time you learn a new noun learn it with both the article and the plural form. It is easier to memorize.

Plural noun endings as indicated in this book:

(-)	der Hamster, die Hamster	(no change)
(¨)	die Mutter, die Mütter	(Umlaut)
(e)	der Schuh, die Schuhe	(ending e)
(¨e)	der Gast, die Gäste	(Umlaut + e)
(er)	das Schild, die Schilder	(ending er)
(¨er)	das Fass, die Fässer	(Umlaut + er)
(n)	die Farbe, die Farben	(ending n)
(en)	die Frau, die Frauen	(ending en)
(s)	das Radio, die Radios	(ending s)

The plural of most feminine German nouns is created by adding -**en** or -**n**: die Schule, die Schulen; die Fahrkarte, die Fahrkarten.

Nouns that add -**s** in the plural are mainly of foreign origin or are words that end in a vowel: der Job, die Jobs; das Hobby, die Hobbies; das Auto, die Autos; die Oma, die Omas.

Some plural forms are identical to the singular: der Wagen, die Wagen; der Ellbogen, die Ellbogen; der Computer, die Computer.

Pronouns

Nominative (subject)

Singular		Plural	
I	ich	*we*	wir
you	du	*you*	ihr
he	er	*they*	sie
she	sie	*you*	Sie (formal)
it	es		

Other cases

Pronouns in German change according to their function in the sentence, just as they do in English, when *I* changes to *me*, *she* to *her*, etc.:

> *I* went by train to London. My friends took *me* home in their car.
> *She* really enjoys reading. I saw *her* in the library.

Singular				Plural			
acc (object*)		dat (indirect object*)		acc (object*)		dat (indirect object*)	
me	mich	*(to) me*	mir	*us*	uns	*(to) us*	uns
you	dich	*(to) you*	dir	*you*	euch	*(to) you*	euch
him	ihn	*(to) him*	ihm				
her	sie	*(to) her*	ihr	} *them*	sie	} *(to) them*	ihnen
it	es	*(to) it*	ihm				
				you (formal) Sie		*(to) you*	Ihnen

*and after certain prepositions

Note: there are three words for *you* in German: **du** (informal) for family members, relatives, good friends and among students; **Sie** (formal); **ihr** (informal) to a group of people.

Remember: sie is used three times: **sie** (*she*), **sie** (*they*) and, finally, **Sie** (with a capital letter) (formal form for *you*).

Remember to use **Sie** in general for people over the age of 16. (For further details see notes in Unit 1.)

Articles/determiners

Definite article: the

The word for *the* is **der** (m), **die** (f), **das** (n) or **die** (pl) in the nominative. **Der** changes in the accusative to **den** (m). All articles change in the dative: **dem** (m), **der** (f), **dem** (n), **den** (pl).

	Singular			Plural
	m	f	n	
nom	**der** Mann	**die** Frau	**das** Kind	**die** Männer
acc	**den** Mann	**die** Frau	**das** Kind	**die** Männer
dat	**dem** Mann	**der** Frau	**dem** Kind	**den** Männern

The genitive is **des** Mannes, **der** Frau, **des** Kindes, **der** Männer.

Remember: the subject of the sentence is in the *nominative*, the direct object of the sentence is in the *accusative*, the indirect object is in the *dative*.

Nominative

The woman lives in Berlin.
('The woman' is the subject of the sentence, and therefore in the nominative.)
Die Frau wohnt in Berlin.

Accusative

Can you see the man who is working in the street?
('The man' is the direct object of the sentence, and therefore in the accusative.)
Siehst du **den** Mann, der in der Straße arbeitet?

Dative

Give the book to the child!
('The child' is the indirect object of the sentence, and therefore in the dative.)
Geben Sie das Buch **dem** Kind!

Give the books to the children!
('The children' is the indirect object of the sentence, and therefore in the dative.)
Geben Sie die Bücher **den** Kindern!

Prepositions

The articles (*the, a* etc.) also change after prepositions: see page 16.

Indefinite article: a/an, and possessive adjectives

The word for *a/an* is **ein/eine/einen/einem**; for *my*: **mein/meine/meinen/meinem**.

	Singular			Plural
	f	m	n	
my	**meine** Tante	**mein** Onkel	**mein** Kind	**meine** Kinder
your	**deine** Tante	**dein** Onkel	**dein** Kind	**deine** Kinder
his	**seine** Tante	**sein** Onkel	**sein** Kind	**seine** Kinder
her	**ihre** Tante	**ihr** Onkel	**ihr** Kind	**ihre** Kinder
our	**unsere** Tante	**unser** Onkel	**unser** Kind	**unsere** Kinder
your	**eure** Tante	**euer** Onkel	**euer** Kind	**eure** Kinder
your	**Ihre** Tante	**Ihr** Onkel	**Ihr** Kind	**Ihre** Kinder

Meine Landkarte ist verschwunden. *My map has disappeared.*
Mein Radio ist kaputt. *My radio is broken.*
Mein Auto ist sehr alt. *My car is very old.*

Seine Tante wohnt in Köln. *His aunt lives in Cologne.*
Sein Onkel kommt aus Leipzig. *His uncle comes from Leipzig.*
Ihr Enkelkind lebt in Hamburg. *Her grandchild lives in Hamburg.*

Remember: her = ihr/e; Ihr/e with a capital letter is *your* (formal)
Example: Ich gebe **ihr ihre** Tasche. *I give her her handbag.*

Ich möchte gerne **Ihre** Tochter treffen. *I would like to meet your daughter.*

A/**ein**, *my*/**mein**, *your*/**dein**, *his*/**sein**, *her*/**ihr**, *your*/**euer**, *our*/**unser**, *no*, *any*/**kein**.

	Singular			Plural
	m	**f**	**n**	
nom	**ein** Bruder	**eine** Schwester	**ein** Baby	**keine** Kinder
acc	**einen** Bruder	**eine** Schwester	**ein** Baby	**keine** Kinder
dat	**einem** Bruder	**einer** Schwester	**einem** Baby	**keinen** Kindern
gen	**eines** Bruders	**einer** Schwester	**eines** Babys	**keiner** Kinder

Ein Bruder von mir studiert zur Zeit in Frankfurt.
One of my brothers is studying in Frankfurt at present.

Ich habe **einen** Bruder und **eine** Schwester.
I have a brother and a sister.

Lass uns in **ein** schönes Restaurant gehen.
Let us go to a nice restaurant.

In German there is also a word for '*not a*' (see section on negative expressions later, page 26).

This/these

	Singular			Plural
	m	f	n	
nom	**dieser** Mantel	**diese** Jacke	**dieses** Kleid	**diese** Schuhe
acc	**diesen** Mantel	**diese** Jacke	**dieses** Kleid	**diese** Schuhe
dat	**diesem** Mantel	**dieser** Jacke	**diesem** Kleid	**diesen** Schuhen

Nominative
Dieser Mantel steht ihr gut.
Diese Jacke steht ihr gut.
Dieses Kleid steht ihr gut.
Diese Schuhe stehen ihr gut.

Accusative
Ich trage **diesen** Mantel gerne.
Ich trage **diese** Jacke gerne.
Ich trage **dieses** Kleid gerne.
Ich trage **diese** Schuhe gerne.

Dative
Zu **diesem** Mantel trage ich einen Hut.
Zu **dieser** Jacke trage ich einen Hut.
Zu **diesem** Kleid trage ich einen Hut.
Zu **diesen** Schuhen trage ich Hosen.

Prepositions

The article changes when it is used after certain prepositions, e.g. **bis, durch, für, gegen, ohne, um, wider** are followed by *the accusative*:

Das Buch ist für **den** Studenten. *The book is for the student.*
Das Auto fuhr gegen **den** Baum. *The car crashed into the tree.*
Fahren Sie durch **den** Tunnel. *Drive through the tunnel.*

The preposition **entlang** (*along*) also changes the article to the *accusative*, but it follows the noun:

Ich fuhr den Kurfürstendamm   *I drove along the*
  entlang.   *Kurfürstendamm.*

The following prepositions are *always* followed by the d[ative]
aus, außer, bei, gegenüber, mit, nach, seit, von, zu:

Ich hole das Buch aus **dem** Auto. *I get the book from th[e car.]*
Sie hat außer **der** Schwester keine Verwandten. *She doe[s not]*
have any relatives apart from her sister.
Er wohnt bei **seiner** Tante. *He lives with his aunt.*
Wir fahren mit **dem** Bus. *We are going by bus.*
Nach **dem** Theater sollten wir in eine Kneipe gehen. *After the*
theatre we should go to a pub.
Seit **dem** Unfall auf der Autobahn fahre ich langsamer. *Since*
the accident on the motorway, I drive more slowly.
Sie hat den Stadtplan von **einer** Tankstelle. *She got the street*
map from a petrol station.
Ich gehe zu **dem** kleinen Laden um die Ecke. *I go to the small*
shop around the corner.

For examples of prepositions following verbs, and of
prepositions taking the dative or the accusative, depending on
whether they indicate motion or position, see pages 67–70.

Verbs

Infinitives and present tense

There is one way of expressing the present tense in German,
while in English there are three:

I live in ...	ich lebe in ...
I am living in ...	ich lebe in ...
I do live in ...	ich lebe in ...

In English the infinitive of a verb is always preceded by 'to' (*to
go/to eat*). In German the verb consists of the stem + the ending
-en:

wohn + **en** = wohnen
kauf + **en** = kaufen
fahr + **en** = fahren

A few others end in **-ern** or **-n**:

kümm + **ern** = kümmern
fütt + **ern** = füttern

For regular verbs in the present tense the following endings are added to the stem:

ich	ends in	e	ich wohne in Berlin
du		st	du wohnst in Berlin
er		t	er wohnt in Berlin
sie		t	sie wohnt in Berlin
es		t	es wohnt in Berlin
wir		en	wir wohnen in Berlin
ihr		t	ihr wohnt in Berlin
sie		en	sie wohnen in Berlin
Sie		en	Sie wohnen in Berlin

Note: Wir/*we* and sie/Sie/*they* take the same ending: **en**.

There are some irregular verbs. The easiest way is to learn these by heart when you come across them, e.g. *to eat*, **essen**: ich esse, du isst, er/sie/es isst, wir essen, ihr esst, sie essen, Sie essen; **fahren**: *to drive/go travel*, ich fahre, du fährst, er/sie/es fährt, wir fahren, ihr fahrt, sie fahren, Sie fahren.

Auxiliary verbs *to have* and *to be*

i Useful verbs to learn: *to have*, **haben** and *to be*, **sein**. You will use them constantly, so learn them by heart from the beginning.

to be	**sein**
I am	ich bin
you are	du bist
he is	er ist
she is	sie ist
it is	es ist
we are	wir sind
you are	ihr seid
they are	sie sind
you are	Sie sind

to have	**haben**
I have	ich habe
you have	du hast
he has	er hat
she has	sie hat
it has	es hat
we have	wir haben
you have	ihr habt
they have	sie haben
you have	Sie haben

Some commonly used verbs are: **arbeiten, gehen, fahren, kaufen, machen** and **spielen**:

	to work	to go	to drive	to buy	to make/do	to play
ich	arbeite	gehe	fahre	kaufe	mache	spiele
du	arbeitest	gehst	fährst	kaufst	machst	spielst
er/sie/es	arbeitet	geht	fährt	kauft	macht	spielt
wir	arbeiten	gehen	fahren	kaufen	machen	spielen
ihr	arbeitet	geht	fahrt	kauft	macht	spielt
sie	arbeiten	gehen	fahren	kaufen	machen	spielen
Sie	arbeiten	gehen	fahren	kaufen	machen	spielen

	to know	to know	to eat	to see	to be called
ich	weiß	kenne	esse	sehe	heiße
du	weißt	kennst	isst	siehst	heißt
er/sie /es	weiß	kennt	isst	sieht	heißt
wir	wissen	kennen	essen	sehen	heißen
ihr	wisst	kennt	esst	seht	heißt
sie	wissen	kennen	essen	sehen	heißen
Sie	wissen	kennen	essen	sehen	heißen

Note: The difference between **wissen** and **kennen**. You use **kennen** to express you know a person or place: **Ich kenne Frau Meier. Ich kenne Berlin.** But you know *something*: **Ich weiß das.** (*I know that.*) **Ich weiß, dass er morgen kommt.** (*I know that he is coming tomorrow.*)

Here are some more commonly used verbs:

to *answer*	antworten, ich antworte
to *arrive*	<u>an</u>kommen*, ich komme <u>an</u>
to *ask*	fragen, ich frage
to *be able to*	können, ich kann
to *bring/fetch*	bringen, ich bringe
to *call* (phone)	<u>an</u>rufen*, ich rufe <u>an</u>
to *cancel*	<u>ab</u>sagen*, ich sage <u>ab</u>
to *find*	finden, ich finde
to *forget*	vergessen, ich vergesse
to *go in*	<u>rein</u>gehen*, ich gehe <u>rein</u>
to *go out*	<u>raus</u>gehen*, ich gehe <u>raus</u>
to *have to*	müssen, ich muss
to *know* (somebody)	kennen, ich kenne

to *know how to*	wissen, ich weiß
to *leave*	verlassen, ich verlasse
to *look for*	suchen, ich suche
to *need*	brauchen, ich brauche
to *pay*	bezahlen, ich bezahle
to *regret*	bereuen, ich bereue
to *remember*	erinnern, ich erinnere
to *reserve*	reservieren, ich reserviere
to *see*	sehen, ich sehe
to *study*	studieren, ich studiere
to *take*	nehmen, ich nehme
to *want/would like to*	möchten, ich möchte
to *write*	schreiben, ich schreibe

*These are *separable* verbs. As you can see, the *separable prefix* (underlined) is split from the verb when it is used in the present tense (and certain other tenses). In the infinitive and in past tenses with **haben** and **sein** it is prefixed: see pages 20–22. Throughout this book, underlining of a prefix in a verb indicates that this is a separable verb.

Talking about the past

In spoken German, the perfect tense is generally used instead of the imperfect. The perfect tense comprises the auxiliary verb **haben** or **sein** and the *past participle*:

> Ich habe ein Buch gelesen. *I read a book.*
> Ich habe in Deutschland gewohnt. *I lived in Germany.*

> Ich bin nach London geflogen. *I flew to London.*
> Ich bin ins Kino gegangen. *I went to the cinema.*

Verbs with *haben*

ℹ 70% of all verbs take **haben** (*to have*). Only 30% take **sein** (*to be*).

The following common verbs form the perfect tense with **haben**:

> to *achieve* erreichen: *I achieved my goal.* Ich habe mein Ziel erreicht.
> to *answer* beantworten: *I answered the question.* Ich habe die Frage beantwortet.
> to *ask* fragen: *I asked for the bill.* Ich habe nach der Rechnung gefragt.

to attend   teilnehmen: *I attended the meeting.*   Ich habe an der Besprechung teilgenommen.

to buy   kaufen: *I bought a new car.*   Ich habe ein neues Auto gekauft.

to complete   vervollständigen: *I completed the puzzle.*   Ich habe das Puzzle vervollständigt.

to do   tun: *I did that.*   Ich habe das getan.

to drink   trinken: *I drank too much coffee.*   Ich habe zu viel Kaffee getrunken.

to eat   essen: *I did not eat anything.*   Ich habe nichts gegessen.

to hear   hören: *I heard a loud noise.*   Ich habe ein lautes Geräusch gehört.

to listen to   zuhören: *I listened to the announcement.*   Ich habe der Ansage zugehört.

to read   lesen: *I read an interesting book.*   Ich habe ein interessantes Buch gelesen.

to say   sagen: *I did not say anything.*   Ich habe nichts gesagt.

to sleep   schlafen: *I slept until 8 o'clock.*   Ich habe bis 8 Uhr geschlafen.

to take   nehmen: *I took the next train.*   Ich habe den nächsten Zug genommen.

to talk   sprechen: *I talked to him briefly.*   Ich habe kurz mit ihm gesprochen.

to think   denken: *I thought about him.*   Ich habe an ihn gedacht.

to write   schreiben: *I wrote him an email.*   Ich habe ihm eine E-Mail geschrieben.

Verbs with *sein*

ℹ All verbs of motion take **sein** (*to be*).

Some examples: *to go*, **gehen**; *to drive/travel/go*, **fahren**; *to fly*, **fliegen**; *to swim*, **schwimmen**; *to come*, **kommen**; *to jog*, **joggen**.

Wir **sind** mit dem Auto nach Berlin **gefahren**. *We took the car to Berlin.*

Wir **sind** in die Stadt **gegangen**. *We went into town.*

Wir **sind** nach Sylt **geflogen**. *We flew to Sylt.*

Er **ist** 10 Bahnen **geschwommen**. *He swam 10 lengths.*

Sie **ist** gestern Abend in die Kneipe **gekommen**. *She came to the pub last night.*

Remember: The verbs to *stay*, **bleiben**, and *to be*, **sein**, take **sein**: (*I stayed in Germany for three weeks.*) Ich **bin** drei Wochen in Deutschland **geblieben**.

Verbs expressing a change of state:

Ich bin <u>auf</u>gewacht	*I woke up*
Er ist gestorben	*He died*
Ich bin <u>ein</u>geschlafen	*I fell asleep*

Reflexive verbs

to amuse   sich amüsieren: *I amused myself in the cinema.* Ich habe mich im Kino amüsiert.

to film   sich filmen: *We filmed ourselves in front of the Brandenburger Tor.* Wir haben uns vor dem Brandenburger Tor gefilmt.

to get on   sich verstehen: *I got on really well with him.* Ich habe mich mit ihm wirklich gut verstanden.

to hurry   sich beeilen: *I hurried to get the bus.* Ich habe mich beeilt um den Bus zu bekommen.

to introduce   sich vorstellen: *He introduced me to his sister.* Er hat mich seiner Schwester vorgestellt.

to meet   sich treffen: *They met at the tourist office.* Sie haben sich am Verkehrsbüro getroffen.

to meet again   sich <u>wieder</u>treffen: *They met again at the train station.* Sie haben sich am Bahnhof <u>wieder</u>getroffen.

to see again   sich <u>wieder</u>sehen: *They saw each other again the next day.* Sie haben sich am nächsten Tag <u>wieder</u>gesehen.

to shower   sich duschen: *I took a shower at 9 o'clock.* Ich habe mich um 9 Uhr geduscht.

to sit down   sich setzen: *I sat down beside my colleague.* Ich habe mich neben meine Kollegin gesetzt.

Imperfect tense

You use the imperfect mainly to write a report or talk about an event in a more formal way. Very common in the spoken language, however, are the words: **war** (*was*), **hatte** (*had*), **musste** (*had to*), **konnte** (*was able to*), **wollte** (*wanted to*).

I was:	ich war, du warst, er/sie es war
	wir waren, ihr wart, sie waren, Sie waren

I had:	ich hatte, du hattest, er/sie/es hatte
	wir hatten, ihr hattet, sie hatten, Sie hatten
I had to:	ich musste, du musstest, er/sie/es musste
	wir mussten, ihr musstet, sie mussten, Sie
	mussten
I could:	ich konnte, du konntest, er/sie/es konnte
	wir konnten, ihr konntet, sie konnten, Sie
	konnten
I wanted to:	ich wollte, du wolltest, er/sie/es wollte
	wir wollten, ihr wolltet, sie wollten, Sie wollten

Es war ein wunderschöner Urlaub. *It was a wonderful holiday.*

Das Wetter war sehr gut. *The weather was very good.*

Wir hatten einen sehr angenehmen Flug. *We had a very pleasant flight.*

Mussten Sie lange warten? *Did you have to wait long?*

Konnten Sie in dem Zug schlafen? *Were you able to sleep in the train?*

Other verbs in the imperfect:

	flew	*came*	*wrote*	*went*	*learnt*	*studied*
ich	flog	kam	schrieb	ging	lern**te**	studier**te**
du	flogst	kamst	schriebst	gingst	lern**test**	studier**test**
er/sie/es	flog	kam	schrieb	ging	lern**te**	studier**te**
wir	flogen	kamen	schrieben	gingen	lern**ten**	studier**ten**
ihr	flogt	kamt	schriebt	gingt	lern**tet**	studier**tet**
sie	flogen	kamen	schrieben	gingen	lern**ten**	studier**ten**
Sie	flogen	kamen	schrieben	gingen	lern**ten**	studier**ten**

Er schlief im Flugzeug. *He slept in the plane.*

Sie gingen mit dem Manager zu einer Besprechung. *They went to a meeting with the manager.*

Ich flog nach Köln. *I flew to Cologne.*

Es war kalt/warm. *It was cold/hot.*

Ich musste zu dem Termin gehen. *I had to go to the appointment.*

Er sprach zu den Zuschauern. *He was talking to the audience.*

Ich sprach mit dem Mann. *I was talking to the man.*

Talking about the future

The future tense is formed with the auxiliary verb **werden** and the *infinitive*:

> Ich werde nach Hamburg fliegen. *I am flying to Hamburg.*
> Ich werde ein Auto mieten. *I am going to rent a car.*
> Wir werden unsere Verwandten besuchen. *We will visit our relatives.*

i There is, however, an easy way of talking about events in the future, as you can use the *present tense* to indicate when you are going to do something: i.e. *In summer I am (I shall be) going to Switzerland.* Ich **fahre** im Sommer in die Schweiz.

Use the present tense when it is obvious that you are going to do something:

> *Are you going to take the bus?* **Nehmen** Sie/**nimmst** du den Bus?
> *I will be taking the bus.* Ich nehme den Bus.

Useful phrases in the future (both forms):

> *I will go (in two hours).* Ich werde (in zwei Stunden) gehen/ ich gehe in zwei Stunden. *Will you be going to the meeting?* Werden Sie zu der Besprechung gehen? *Will you be going to the meeting this afternoon?* Gehen Sie heute Nachmittag zu der Besprechung?
> *I will be there.* Ich werde da sein. *I will be there (tomorrow).* Ich bin (morgen) da.
> *I will do that.* Ich werde es machen. *I will do that today.* Ich mache es (heute).
> *Will you do it?* Werden Sie/Wirst du es es machen? *Will you do it (next week)?* Machen Sie/Machst du es (nächste Woche)?
> *Will you take the bus?* Werden Sie/Wirst du den Bus nehmen? Nehmen Sie/Nimmst du den Bus ?
> *How will you go?* Wie werden Sie/wirst du fahren? Wie fahren Sie/fährst du?
> *When will you arrive?* Wann werden Sie/wirst du <u>an</u>kommen? Wann kommen Sie/kommst du <u>an</u>?
> *When will you leave?* Wann fahren Sie/fährst du <u>ab</u>? Wann werden Sie/wirst du <u>ab</u>fahren?
> *What will the weather be like?* Wie wird das Wetter sein?
> *How much will it cost?* Was kostet es? Was wird es kosten?
> *Will it be suitable for children?* Wird es für Kinder geeignet sein? Ist es für Kinder geeignet?

What will he do? Was wird er machen? Was macht er
   (morgen)?
What will he have? Was wird er haben?
What will you take? Was werden Sie/wirst du <u>mit</u>nehmen?
   Was nehmen Sie/nimmst du <u>mit</u>?
When will it be? Wann wird es sein? Wann ist es?
Is it going to rain (tomorrow)? Wird es regnen? Regnet es
   morgen?
It will probably rain. Es wird wahrscheinlich regnen. Es
   regnet wahrscheinlich.
Will there be much traffic? Gibt es viel Verkehr da? Wird es
   viel Verkehr geben?

Conditional and subjunctive

Conditional

The conditional is formed with the auxiliary verb **würden** plus
the *infinitive*. It corresponds to the English pattern verb plus
infinitve.

I would like to go to the park. Ich würde gerne in den Park
   gehen.
I would appreciate it if you came with me. Ich würde es
   schätzen, wenn du mit mir kommen würdest.
I would come along. Ich würde <u>mit</u>kommen.
I would go to view the castle. Ich würde das Schloss
   besichtigen gehen.
It would be Monday. Es würde Montag werden.
I would have it on Friday. Ich würde es am Freitag haben.
I would do that. Ich würde das tun.
He would buy the shoes if they were cheaper. Er würde die
   Schuhe kaufen, wenn sie billiger wären.
Would you buy this house? Würdest du dieses Haus kaufen?
Would you go there? Würden Sie dorthin gehen?
Would you go with me to the cinema. Würden Sie mit mir ins
   Kino gehen?

i It is very common to use the conditional as a polite request:
würden Sie/würdest du ...:

Würden Sie mir bitte aus dem Mantel helfen! *Would please help
   me out of my coat!*
Würden Sie mir bitte sagen wie spät es ist! *Would you please tell
   me what time it is!*

Würdet ihr bitte ruhig sein! *Would you please be quiet!*
Würden Sie das bitte nehmen! *Would you please take that!*
Würden Sie bitte das Formular <u>unter</u>schreiben! *Would you please sign that form!*

Subjunctive

There are two forms of the subjunctive: the general subjunctive and the special subjunctive. The general subjunctive is more common and falls into the following categories: wishes and hopes: **bleib gesund/bleiben Sie gesund** (*stay healthy*); **mögen Sie glücklich sein** (*may you be happy*); **mögest du gesund werden** (*may you be well again*).

The second form of the subjunctive is used for: **if** sentences after **als ob** and **if** sentences after **wenn...** (hypothetical):

Er sah aus, als ob er nichts verstanden hätte. *He looked as if he had not understood a thing.*
Es sieht so aus, als ob es regnen würde. *It looks as if it is going to rain.*
Er tut so, als ob er es könnte. *He pretends that* (lit: *as if*) *he could do that.*
Wenn ich mehr Geld hätte, würde ich eine Weltreise machen. *If I had more money I would travel around the world.*
Wenn ich Sie/du wäre, würde ich das tun. *If I were you I would do that.*
Wenn ich könnte, würde ich es machen. *If I could I would do it.*

Negative expressions

How to say you don't do/don't like something

Remember: you use **mögen** in connection with a noun:

Ich mag keine Pizza. (*I don't like pizza.*)

But: use **gerne** with a verb: Ich studiere nicht gerne. (*I don't like to study*).

Ich tanze nicht gerne. *I don't like to dance.*
Ich mag ... nicht. *I don't like ...*
Ich mag das nicht. *I don't like that.*
Ich ... nicht gerne. *I don't like ...*
Ich singe nicht gerne. *I don't like singing.*

Use **kein** in front of a noun:

> Ich mag kein Fleisch. *I don't like meat.*
> Ich esse kein Fleisch. *I don't eat meat.*
> Mein Freund hat kein Auto. *My friend doesn't have a car.*
> Ich gucke kein Fernsehen. *I don't watch telly.*

Use **nicht** with a verb:

> Ich rauche nicht. *I don't smoke.*
> Ich tanze nicht. *I don't dance.*
> Sie ruft mich nicht an. *She does not phone me.*

Nichts = *anything*:

> Ich mache nichts. *I don't do anything.*
> Ich habe nichts. *I haven't got anything.*
> Nichts ist nicht gut genug. *Nothing is not good enough.*

Nobody/anybody:

> Ich kenne niemanden. *I don't know anyone.*
> Ich habe niemanden gesehen. *I haven't seen anyone.*
> Niemand geht in das Geschäft. *No one goes to that shop.*

Noch nie = *never*:

> Ich bin noch nie in Leipzig gewesen. *I have never been to Leipzig.*
> Er hat noch nie Austern gegessen. *He has never eaten oysters.*
> Wir haben den Film noch nie gesehen. *We have never seen the film.*

Noch nicht = *not yet*:

> Ich habe mit ihr noch nicht gesprochen. *I have not yet spoken to her.*
> Ich habe das Zimmer noch nicht gebucht. *I have not booked the hotel room yet.*
> Der Bus ist noch nicht gekommen. *The bus has not arrived yet.*

Immer noch nicht = *still not*:

> Er hat den Brief immer noch nicht geschrieben. *He still has not written the letter.*
> Der Zug ist immer noch nicht angekommen. *The train has still not arrived.*

Nicht mehr = *any more*:

Ich gehe dort nicht mehr hin. *I don't go there any more.*
Ich werde ihn/sie nicht mehr sehen. *I won't see him/her any more.*
Ich spiele nicht mehr. *I don't play any more.*

Kein = *not any*:

Haben Sie keine Zigaretten mehr? *Do you have any more cigarettes?*
Hast du/Haben Sie keine? *Haven't you got any?*
Nein, ich habe keine. *No, I haven't.*

Nein, ich konnte keinen Termin bekommen. *No, I couldn't get an appointment.*

Other negatives

Haben Sie keinen Tisch gebucht? *Did you not book a table?*
Nein, sie sind nicht ans Telefon gegangen. *No, they didn't answer the phone.*
Sind Sie nicht zur Bank gekommen? *Didn't you get to the bank?*
Nein, sie war nicht geöffnet. *No, it wasn't open.*
Haben Sie nicht/hast du nicht mit ihm gesprochen? *Didn't you speak to him?*
Nein, ich habe mit ihm noch nicht gesprochen. *No, I have not spoken to him yet.*
Haben Sie keine Tickets für die Show bekommen? *Didn't you get any tickets for the show?*
Nein, es gab keine. *No, there weren't any left.*

Haben Sie ihren Freund nicht gesehen? *Didn't you see your friend?*
Er war nicht da. *No, he wasn't in.*

Don't ...!:

No entry	kein Eintritt
No exit	kein Ausgang
No admission	kein Zutritt
No smoking	Nichtraucher
No dogs	keine Hunde
No drinking water	kein Trinkwasser
Don't touch	nicht berühren/nicht <u>an</u>fassen
Don't eat it	nicht essen
Don't open the window	Fenster nicht öffnen

Verboten = *is not allowed/permitted*:

to swim	{ Schwimmen verboten { Baden verboten
to play ball	Ball spielen verboten
to enter	Eintritt verboten
to smoke	Rauchen verboten
the use of mobile phones	Benutzung von Handys ist verboten
to walk on the ice	Betreten der Eisfläche ist verboten

Interrogative – asking questions

You can ask a question by inverting the pronoun and verb:
Haben Sie/hast du ein Auto? *Have you got a new car?*

Sprechen Sie/Sprichst du eine andere Sprache?	*Do you speak another language?*
Fahren Sie/Fährst du nach Frankfurt?	*Do you drive to Frankfurt?*
Haben Sie/Hast du Ihren/ deinen Schlüssel?	*Have you got your key?*
Können Sie/Kannst du mir bitte sagen ...?	*Can you tell me ...?*
Können Sie/Kannst du mir einen Stift leihen?	*Could you lend me a pen?*
Würden Sie/Würdest du gerne <u>mit</u>kommen?	*Would you like to come along?*
Wären es ihnen/Wäre es dir möglich es mir zu erklären?	*Would you be able to explain it to me?*
Sind Sie/Bist du müde?	*Are you tired?*
Sind Sie/Bist du in die Stadt gegangen?	*Did you go to town?*
Haben Sie/Hast du ihn gesehen?	*Have you seen him?*
Haben Sie/Hast du das Steak probiert?	*Did you try the steak?*
Haben Sie/Hast du den Film gesehen?	*Have you seen the film?*
Rauchen Sie/Rauchst du?	*Do you smoke?*
Bevorzugen Sie/Bevorzugst du Rot- oder Weißwein?	*Do you prefer red or white wine?*
Essen Sie/Isst du Fisch?	*Do you eat fish?*

Nehmen Sie/Nimmst du Medikamente?	*Are you taking medication?*
Haben Sie/Hast du ihre Verwandten besucht?	*Have you visited her relatives?*
Studieren Sie/Studierst du im ersten Jahr?	*Are you in your first year* (of study)*?*
Gehen Sie/Gehst du regelmäßig schwimmen?	*Do you regularly go for a swim?*
Braucht man ein Ticket für diese Maschine?	*Do you need a ticket for this machine?*
Brauche ich Kleingeld für den Bus?	*Do I need change for the bus?*
Fahren Sie an der Küste entlang?	*Do you go along the coast?*

Questions asking for information are introduced by a question word:

Who?	wer?	*How?*	wie?
When?	wann?	*How much?*	wie viel?
Where?	wo?	*Whom?*	wen?
Why?	warum?	*To whom?*	wem?
Why?	weshalb?	*From where?*	woher?
What?	was?	*Whose?*	wessen?

Note: Don't mix up *where* with **wer**: *who* is **wer** in German; *where* is **wo**:

Who are you?	Wer sind Sie? Wer bist du?
Where is Mrs Meier?	Wo ist Frau Meier?
How are you?	Wie geht es Ihnen/Wie geht es dir?
How much does the street map cost?	Wie viel kostet der Stadtplan?
How many visitors are expected?	Wie viele Besucher werden erwartet?
How long do we have to wait for the train?	Wie lange müssen wir auf den Zug warten?
Who is Mrs Meier?	Wer ist Frau Meier?
Who are you supposed to be seeing?	Wen sollten Sie eigentlich treffen?
Who gave you permission to do that?	Wer hat Ihnen/dir die Erlaubnis gegeben, das zu tun?
Who arranged it for you?	Wer hat das für Sie/dich **arrangiert?**

Who do you think you are?	Wer glauben Sie, wer Sie sind?
	Wer glaubst du wer du bist?
Whose car is it?	Wessen Auto ist das?
Whose euros are they?	Wessen Euros sind das?
What is wrong/happening?	Was ist los?
What is going on?	Was ist hier los?
What do you want?	Was wollen Sie/Was willst du?
What is the name of your hotel?	Wie ist der Name Ihres Hotels?
What kind of conference are you attending?	Was für eine Konferenz besuchen Sie?
Which floor are you on?	In welchem Stock sind Sie?
Which room are you in?	In welchem Zimmer sind Sie?
Which is your place?	Welcher Platz ist Ihr Platz?
Which is your car?	Welches Auto ist Ihr Auto?
Which is your bag?	Welche Tasche ist Ihre Tasche?

The 16 most common questions when abroad:

What is your name?	Wie ist Ihr/dein Name? Wie heißen Sie/heißt du?
Where are you from?	Woher kommen Sie?
How long are you staying?	Wie lange sind Sie hier?
Where are you staying?	Wo sind Sie <u>unter</u>gebracht?
Have you got your passport?	Haben Sie Ihren Personalausweis?
What do you want?	Was möchten Sie?/Was möchtest du?
Do you speak German?	Sprechen Sie Deutsch?
Do you like it here?	Mögen Sie es hier?
What are you doing here?	Was machen Sie hier?
Could you please write it down for me?	Könnten Sie es bitte für mich <u>auf</u>schreiben ?
Can you spell it please?	Können Sie es bitte buchstabieren?
Can you help me?	Können Sie mir bitte helfen?
When does the train leave?	Wann fährt der Bus <u>ab</u>?
When does the performance start?	Wann fängt die Vorstellung <u>an</u>?
When are we going to meet Mr Schmidt?	Wann treffen wir Herrn Schmidt?
When are we having dinner?	Wann essen wir Abendessen?

i If you wish to be very polite use **könnten** instead of **können**:

Könnten Sie das bitte wiederholen.	*Could you please repeat that.*
Könnten Sie mir bitte helfen?	*Could please help me?*
Könnte ich bitte meinen Schlüssel haben?	*Could I please have my key?*

Adjectives

An adjective describes a noun or a pronoun. When an adjective is used *after* the noun, the adjective ending does not change, e.g. **Das Auto ist *blau*.** (*The car is blue.*) If the adjective is before the noun it does change, however, e.g, **Das blaue Auto ist neu.**

There are only two different endings for adjectives following the definitive articles, **der, die, das** and **dieser, jener, jeder** and **welcher.** The endings are -e and -en:

Ich kaufe den neuen Mantel.
Dieser neue Mantel gefällt mir gut.
Welcher blaue Hut passt gut zu dem neuen Mantel?
Die neuen Mäntel gefallen mir gut.

	Singular			Plural
	m	f	n	
nom	-e	-e	-e	-en
acc	-en	-e	-e	-en
dat	-en	-en	-en	-en
gen	-en	-en	-en	-en

Adjective endings after the indefinite article, **ein** (*a*), **mein** (*my*), **dein** (*your*), etc.:

	Singular			Plural
	m	f	n	
nom	-er	-e	-es	-en
acc	-en	-e	-es	-en
dat	-en	-en	-en	-en
gen	-en	-en	-en	-en

Ich kaufe einen großen Stadtplan.
Ein großer Stadtplan ist sehr nützlich.
Ich gebe den großen Stadtplan meiner kleinen Schwester.

Auf dem Marktplatz gibt es eine neue Eisdiele.
Eine andere alte Eisdiele ist um die Ecke.
Ich gehe gerne in eine große Eisdiele.
In einer großen Eisdiele gibt es viele verschiedene Eissorten.

Useful words for describing people:

groß	*tall*	klein	*small*
dünn	*thin*	dick	*fat*
glücklich	*happy*	unglücklich	*unhappy*
ruhig	*quiet*	laut	*loud*
schüchtern	*shy*	selbstbewusst	*self-confident*
entspannt	*relaxed*	gestresst	*stressed*
zurückhaltend	*laid back*	fordernd	*demanding*
ichbezogen	*self-centred*	hilfsbereit	*giving*
selbstsüchtig	*selfish*	selbstlos	*selfless*
egoistisch	*egoistic*	rücksichtsvoll	*considerate*
aktiv	*active*	faul	*lazy*
gut aussehend	*good looking*	hässlich	*ugly*
fröhlich	*cheerful*	bedrückt	*depressed*
intelligent	*intelligent*	dumm	*stupid*
modern	*modern*	konservativ	*conservative*
gepflegt	*smart*	ungepflegt	*scruffy*
artig	*well-behaved*	ungezogen	*naughty*
erotisch	*erotic*	prüde	*prudish*
höflich	*polite*	unhöflich	*rude*
selbstbewusst	*self-confident*	unsicher	*uncertain*
entschlossen	*determined*	unentschlossen	*undecided*
schickimicki	*sloaney*	lässig	*casual*
ehrlich	*honest*	unehrlich	*dishonest*

i False friends: Be **careful not** to translate *sensible* by **sensibel** or *sympathetic* by **sympathisch**.

sympathisch	*pleasant, likeable*
verständnissvoll	*sympathetic*
sensibel	*sensitive*
vernünftig	*sensible*
seriös	*respectable*
ernsthaft	*serious*

Ernsthaft?	*Are you serious?*
Seien Sie/Sei ernst!	*Be serious!*
Seien Sie/Sei vernünftig!	*Be sensible!*
Sie ist eine verständnisvolle Person.	*She is a sympathetic person.*

i Young people in Germany use the following 'modern' expressions:

Ich bin total relaxed.	*I am totally relaxed.*
Der Typ ist cool.	*This guy is cool.*
Ich finde das cool.	*I think that's cool.*
Sei nicht so gestresst.	*Don't be so stressed out.*
Das ist ein cooles Auto.	*That's a cool car.*
Meine Arbeit ist zur Zeit wirklich heavy.	*My work is heavy at the moment.*
Das ist powerful.	*That's powerful.*

Some useful words for describing things:

alt	*old*	neu	*new*
gut	*good*	schlecht	*bad*
billig	*cheap*	teuer	*expensive*
schnell	*fast*	langsam	*slow*
in Ordnung	*in good condition*	kaputt	*damaged*
dünn	*flimsy*	fest	*solid*
rauh	*rough*	glatt	*smooth*
glänzend	*shiny*	matt	*dull*
bequem	*comfortable*	unbequem	*uncomfortable*
breit	*wide/broad*	schmal	*narrow*
lang	*long*	kurz	*short*
dünn	*thin*	dick	*thick*
hart	*hard*	weich	*soft*
hoch	*high*	niedrig	*low*
leicht	*light*	schwer	*heavy*
sauber	*clean*	schmutzig	*dirty*
schwer	*heavy*	leicht	*light*
zerbrechlich	*fragile*	stabil	*sturdy*

Comparative and superlative

The comparative is made by adding **-er** to the base form of the adjective, e.g. *small*, **klein**, *smaller*, **klein**er; *wide*, **weit**, *wider*, **weit**er.

Some adjectives need an Umlaut for the comparative as well as for the superlative: *old*, **alt**, *older*, **älter**, *oldest*, **am ältesten**; *often*, **oft**, **öfter**, **am öftesten**.

The superlative is made by adding *am* and ending *-(e)sten*: *tallest*, *am* **größten**; *smallest*, *am* **kleinsten**:

bad schlecht	*worse* schlechter	*worst am* schlechtesten
big groß	*bigger* größer	*biggest am* größten
dear teuer	*dearer* teurer	*dearest am* teuersten
easy leicht	*easier* leichter	*easiest am* leichesten
firm fest	*firmer* fester	*firmest am* festesten
good gut	*better* besser	*best am* besten
late später	*later* später	*latest am* spätesten
little wenig	*less* weniger	*least am* wenigsten
old alt	*older* älter	*oldest am* ältesten
small klein	*smaller* kleiner	*smallest am* kleinsten
tall groß	*taller* größer	*tallest am* größten

But irregular (in German as they are in English!):

much viel	*more* mehr	*most* am meisten
good gut	*better* besser	*best* am besten
much viel	*more* mehr	*most* am meisten

Colours and sizes

Colours *die Farben*

beige	beige
black	schwarz
blue	blau
brown	braun
green	grün
grey	grau
golden	gold
lilac	lila
mauve	malvenfarben
natural	naturfarben
orange	orange
pink	rosa
purple	purpur
red	rot
silver	silber
turquoise	türkis
violet	violett
white	weiss
yellow	gelb

Remember: Write all two-colour adjectives as one word: *dark green*, **dunkelgrün**; *dark red*, **dunkelrot**; *bright red*, **knallrot**; *pitch black*, **pechschwarz**; *blue-grey*, **blaugrau**; *silver grey*, **silbergrau**; *light blue*, **hellblau**; *light green*, **hellgrün**.

Remember: Hell can also mean *bright*: **Das Licht ist hell.** (*The light is bright.*)

More colours

salmon pink	lachsrot
khaki	khakifarben
burgundy	burgunderrot
royal blue	königsblau
dark blue	dunkelblau
navy blue	marineblau
pale green	blassgrün
dark green	dunkelgrün
olive green	olivengrün
emerald green	smaragdgrün
bottle green	flaschengrün
grass green	grasgrün
bright red	hellrot
scarlet	scharlachrot
pale yellow	blassgelb
bright yellow	knallgelb
emerald	smaragdfarben
ruby	rubinrot
ruby coloured	weinrot
turquoise	türkis

Sizes

sehr klein	*very small*	klein	*small*
mittelgroß	*medium*	durchschnittlich	*average*
groß	*large*	sehr groß	*very large*
weit	*wide*	schmal	*narrow*
lang	*long*	kurz	*short*
zu lang	*too long*	etwas zu lang	*a bit too long*
viel zu lang	*far too long*	viel zu groß/klein	*far too big/short*

Adverbs

schnell	*quickly*
langsam	*slowly*
zu schnell	*too fast*
gut	*well*

Kommen Sie schnell!	*Come quickly!*
Fahren Sie langsam!	*Drive slowly!*

Sie sind zu schnell gefahren.	*You drove too fast.*
Das haben Sie gut gemacht.	*You did that well.*
Das haben Sie gut ausgesprochen.	*You pronounced that well.*

sofort	*immediately*
total	*completely*
plötzlich	*suddenly*
geräuschlos	*noiselessly*
schmerzhaft	*painfully*
schmerzlos	*painlessly*
glücklicherweise	*happily*
ungefähr	*approximately*
technisch	*technically*
traurigerweise	*sadly*

Die Polizei kommt sofort.	*The police are coming immediately.*
Ich habe das total vergessen.	*I totally forgot about it.*
Plötzlich fing es an zu regnen.	*Suddenly it started to rain.*
Glücklicherweise fährt die Fähre alle zwei Stunden.	*Luckily the ferry goes every two hours.*

sehr	*very*
wenig	*a little*
mehr	*more*
am meisten	*most*
weniger	*less*

Wir treffen uns …:	*We meet …:*
selten	*rarely*
gelegentlich	*occasionally*
regelmäßig	*regularly*
manchmal	*sometimes*
oft	*often*
sehr oft	*very often*
bald	*soon*
nie	*never*
Wir haben uns schon einmal getroffen.	*We have met already.*
schon einmal	*already*
noch nie	*never*
Wir haben uns noch nie getroffen.	*We never met before.*
Wir haben uns kurz getroffen.	*We met briefly.*

, fastest   schnell, schneller, am schnellsten
ter, best   gut, besser, am besten
worse, worst   schlecht, schlechter, am schlechtesten

| | *then* |
| | *now* |
chher | *afterwards* |
orher | *previously* |
früher | *earlier* |
später | *later* |

vor dem Essen   *before the meal*
nach dem Essen   *after the meal*
um nach ... zu gehen ...   *in order to go to ...*
um das zu lesen ...   *in order to read ...*
während er hier war   *while he was here*
während der Besprechung   *during the meeting*

Sentences with *in order to*

Um nach Dresden zu fahren, müssen wir den Zug um 8 Uhr nehmen.
In order to go to Dresden we have to catch the train at 8 o'clock.
Um rechtzeitig <u>anzukommen</u>, sollten wir jetzt gehen.
In order to arrive in time we should leave now.

Impersonal expressions

all	alles
that is all.	das ist alles.
all inclusive	alles inklusive
every	jede/r
every half hour	jede halbe Stunde
every moment	jeden Moment
none	kein/e
none of us	keiner von uns

Numbers, times, days and dates

Cardinal numbers

0 null	3 drei	6 sechs
1 eins	4 vier	7 sieben
2 zwei	5 fünf	8 acht

9	neun	16	sechzehn	30	dreißig
10	zehn	17	siebzehn	40	vierzig
11	elf	18	achtzehn	50	fünfzig
12	zwölf	19	neunzehn	60	sechzig
13	dreizehn	20	zwanzig	70	siebzig
14	vierzehn	21	einundzwanzig	80	achtzig
15	fünfzehn	22	zweiundzwanzig	90	neunzig

Remember: **sechs** but **sechzehn**,
　　　　　sieben but **siebzehn**,
　　　　　dreißig but **zwanzig, vierzig** etc.

Bigger useful numbers:

100	einhundert	1000	eintausend
101	einhundert(und)eins	2000	zweitausend
102	einhundert(und)zwei	2010	zweitausend(und)zehn
110	einhundert(und)zehn	5000	fünftausend
150	einhundert(und)fünfzig	10 000	zehntausend
200	zweihundert	*million*	eine Million
300	dreihundert	*billion*	eine Billion
500	fünfhundert		

Ordinal numbers

first	erste	*fourth*	vierte
second	zweite	*fifth*	fünfte
third	dritte	*tenth*	zehnte
21st	einundzwanzigste		

Some fractions

half	halb	*quarter*	ein Viertel

Dates

the century	das Jahrhundert
1993	neunzehnhundertdreiundneunzig
1994	neunzehnhundertvierundneunzig
the 20th century	das zwanzigste Jahrhundert
the 21st century	das einundzwanzigste Jahrhundert
2002	zweitausend(und)zwei
2003	zweitausend(und)drei
2020	zweitausend(und)zwanzig
the 22nd century	das zweiundzwanzigste Jahrhundert
the millennium	das Millenium

the 1990s	die neunziger Jahre
the year 2003	das Jahr zweitausend(und)drei
the year 2010	das Jahr zweitausend(und)zehn
next year	nächstes Jahr
last year	letztes Jahr
the year before last	das vorletzte Jahr
the coming year	das kommende Jahr

Days and months

Monday	Montag	*Friday*	Freitag
Tuesday	Dienstag	*Saturday*	Samstag/Sonnabend
Wednesday	Mittwoch	*Sunday*	Sonntag
Thursday	Donnerstag		

Note: There are two words for Saturday, **Samstag** and **Sonnabend**. Choose the one you prefer.

January	Januar	*July*	July
February	Februar	*August*	August
March	März	*September*	September
April	April	*October*	Oktober
May	Mai	*November*	November
June	Juni	*December*	Dezember

Expressions of time

second	die Sekunde
minute	die Minute
hour	die Stunde
day	der Tag
week	die Woche
month	der Monat
year	das Jahr
yesterday	gestern
the day before yesterday	vorgestern
today	heute
tomorrow	morgen
the day after tomorrow	übermorgen
morning	der Morgen
afternoon	der Nachmittag
evening	der Abend
night	die Nacht
tonight	heute Abend

Remember: heute Nachmittag, *this afternoon*; heute früh, *this morning*; morgen früh, *tomorrow morning*; gestern Vormittag, *yesterday morning*.

The seasons

spring	der Frühling/das Frühjahr
summer	der Sommer
autumn	der Herbst
winter	der Winter

The clock

Es ist:		
	9.20	neun Uhr zwanzig
	7.10	sieben Uhr zehn
	11.30	elf Uhr dreißig
	12.45	zwölf Uhr fünfundvierzig
	20.35	zwanzig Uhr fünfunddreißig
	21.45	einundzwanzig Uhr fünfundvierzig

Note: You use the 24-hour clock for offical time giving, train/plane leaving times, etc. Otherwise, when asking somebody for the time or making arrangements when to meet, use:

9.00 a.m.	neun Uhr
9.15	viertel nach neun
9.20	zwanzig nach neun
9.30	halb zehn
9.31	neun Uhr einunddreißig
9.40	zwanzig vor zehn
9.45	viertel vor zehn
past	nach
to	vor
a quarter	viertel
half	halb

Remember: halb zehn is *9.30*, halb vier is *3.30*, halb elf is *10.30*.

i When making arrangements to meet somebody, avoid saying the *half ten*, because it can lead to a misunderstanding: If you want to meet someone at half past ten, then it's **halb elf** in German.

half hour	die halbe Stunde
quarter hour	die Viertelstunde
three quarters of an hour	eine Dreiviertelstunde
midnight	Mitternacht
midday	Mittag
sunrise	der Sonnenaufgang
sunset	der Sonnenuntergang

Remember: The same word is used for clock and watch in German: **die Uhr. Meine Uhr ist kaputt.** (*My watch is broken.*) **Es ist 5 Uhr.** (*Es ist 5 o'clock.*)

der Wecker	*alarm clock*
die Armbanduhr	*wristwatch*
die Turmuhr	*clock on a tower*
die Wanduhr	*wall clock*
die Kirchenuhr	*church clock*
die Kuckucksuhr	*cuckoo clock*

There are two expressions that can be used to ask for the time: *what time is it?* **wie spät ist es? wie viel Uhr ist es? Wie spät ist es?** literally means *how late is it?* **Wie viel Uhr ist es?** literally means *how many hours is it?*

Can you give me the time?	Können Sie mir sagen, wie spät es ist?
Can you wake me up at …?	Können Sie mich um … Uhr wecken?
We could meet at 6 o'clock.	Wir könnten uns um 6 Uhr treffen.
Do we want to meet at half seven?	Wollen wir uns um halb acht treffen?
It is late.	Es ist spät.
It is early.	Es ist früh.
It is too late.	Es ist zu spät.
We could meet a bit later.	Wir könnten uns etwas später treffen.
How about a bit later.	Wie wäre es mit etwas später?
My watch does not work any more.	Meine Uhr geht nicht mehr.
My watch is fast/slow.	Meine Uhr geht vor/nach.

Quantity

how heavy?	wie schwer?
weight	das Gewicht
to weigh	wiegen
height	die Höhe
to measure	messen
length	die Länge
content	der Inhalt
volume	das Volumen
to fit in	reinpassen

Weights and measures

how much?	wie viel?
kilo	das Kilo
half a kilo	ein halbes Kilo
500 grams	500 Gramm
a pound	ein Pfund
a litre	ein Liter
a metre	ein Meter
a centimetre	ein Zentimeter
a kilometre	ein Kilometer
a pair	ein Paar
a dozen	ein Dutzend
a slice of	eine Scheibe
a bit more	etwas mehr
a bit less	etwas weniger
how hot?	wie warm?
how cold?	wie kalt?
temperature	die Temperatur
above	über
below	unter
minus	minus
Celsius	das Grad
how fast?	wie schnell?
distance	die Distanz(en), die Entfernung(en)
speed	die Geschwindigkeit(en)
kilometre per hour	der Kilometer/pro Stunde/km/h
mile	die Meile(n)
to drive	fahren
how fast	wie schnell
slowly	langsam
too fast	zu schnell
too slowly	zu langsam
bottle	die Flasche (n)
jar	das Glas (¨er)
tin	die Dose (n)
box	die Schachtel (n)
pot	der Topf (¨e)
coffee pot	die Kaffeekanne (n)
package	die Verpackung (en)

lots of	viele …
little	wenig …
more of	mehr …
full	voll
empty	leer

some honey	ein bisschen Honig
lots of sugar	ganz viel Zucker
hardly any salt	kaum Salz
just a bit of milk	nur ein bisschen Milch
just a drop	nur ein Tropfen

Exclamations, giving orders and being polite

Expressions such as **Entschuldigen Sie (bitte)** (*excuse me please*) or **Entschuldigung** (*sorry*) as well as **danke** and **bitte** are used the same way as in the UK.

But various other meanings of the word **bitte** also occur: when passing something on to somebody it is polite and necessary to say: **hier bitte** or **bitte** or **bitte schön** or **bitte sehr**. All these expressions have a similar meaning to *here you are* but are much politer.

The reply is then **danke** (*thanks*), **ich danke Ihnen** (*thank you*) **ich danke dir, danke schön, vielen Dank** (*many thanks/thanks a lot*). *You are welcome* = **gern geschehen**.

Apart from *please* the word **bitte** has also other meanings:

bitte bitte	*it's a pleasure*
aber bitte	*sure!*
bitte keine Ursache	*it is nothing!*
bitte nur zu	*help yourself!*
na bitte	*there you are!*
aber ich bitte dich/Sie!	*not at all!*
ich bitte darum	*I would be glad if you would …*

Other expressions with **bitte**:

Ich möchte Sie/dich bitten.	*I would like to ask you.*
Ich möchte Sie um etwas bitten.	*I would like to ask you for something.*
Sie können mich um alles bitten.	*You can ask me for anything.*
Fragen Sie mich bitte um nichts.	*Don't ask me for anything.*

Darf ich Sie um Ihren Namen bitten?	*May I asked you for your name?*
bitte nicht	*don't please*
bitte schön (used in a shop as an invitation to you to say what you want)	
danke	*thanks*
vielen Dank	*many thanks*
danke sehr	*thank you*
danke schön	*thank you*
herzlichen Dank	*thank you very much*
danken	*to thank*
dankbar sein	*to be grateful*
sich bedanken für	*to thank for*
Hilfe	*Help!*
Feuer	*Fire!*
Prost/zum Wohl	*Cheers!*
Warten Sie!	*Wait!*
Stop! <u>Anhalten!</u>	*Stop!*
Hören Sie mal! Hör mal!	*Listen!*

Schauen Sie mal! Schau mal!	*Look!* ⎫
Sehen Sie/Sieh mal!	*Look!* ⎬ *Have a look*
Gucken Sie/guck mal!	*Look!* ⎭

Pass me a knife please.	Reichen Sie mir bitte ein Messer.
Fetch a glass.	Holen Sie sich/Hol dir ein Glas.
Take the chocolates.	Nehmen Sie/Nimm die Schokolade.
Bring me my bag.	Bringen Sie/Bring mir meine Tasche.
Order a beer for me.	Bestellen Sie/Bestell mir ein Bier.
Pay for me please.	Bezahlen Sie/Bezahl für mich bitte.
Write it down please.	Schreiben Sie/Schreib es bitte <u>auf</u>.
Spell it please.	Buchstabieren Sie/Buchstabiere es bitte.
Repeat that please.	Wiederholen Sie/Wiederhol das bitte.
Say it again please.	Sagen Sie/Sag es noch einmal.
Try it again.	Probieren Sie/Probier es noch einmal.
Check it again.	Überprüfen Sie/Überprüf es noch mal.

Dialogue

A	Ich lade Sie <u>ein</u>.	*I invite you.*
B	Oh, vielen Dank.	*Many thanks.*
A	Gern geschehen.	*It's a pleasure.*

Excuse me.	Pardon. Entschuldigung.
I'm sorry.	Es tut mir Leid.

Sorry.	Das tut mir Leid.
Excuse me.	Entschuldigen Sie bitte.
I didn't mean it.	Ich wollte das nicht.
I did not know that.	Das wusste ich nicht.
I did not understand that.	Ich habe das nicht verstanden.
Sorry I'm late.	Tut mir Leid für die Verspätung.

When somebody tells you something bad has happened to him/her you respond with: **Das tut mir Leid.**

German spelling quirks

German spelling and pronunciation are much more consistent than English. (See pages 6–9 for more on German pronunciation.)

The vowels

- **a ah** sounds like English *spa*; German: **Tag, Bad, da, haben**
- **a** short **a** sounds like English *cut*; German: **hat**
- **e** at the end of a word sounds like English *get*; German: **Tage, Woche**
- **e eh** long sound; German: **Esel, Elisabeth, Besen**
- **i** short as in English *fish*; German: **ist, Tisch, frisch**
- **i** long **ee** as in English *here*; German: **ihr, immer, finden**
- **o oh** as in English *go, so*; German: **oder, Ober, Dom**
- **u ooh** as in English *June, shoe*; German: **und, Hund, Uhu**

Die Umlaute

- **ä** sounds like English *spare*; German: **Mädchen, März, Kanäle, spät**
- **ö** sounds like English *sir* with round lips; German: **Vögel, schön, mögen**
- **ü** sounds like Scottish pronunciation of *you, shoes*; German: **Müller, müde, früh**
- **eu** sounds like English *boy*; German: **neu, Feuer, teuer**
- **äu** sounds like English *toy*; German: **Häuser, Mäuse**
- **au** sounds like English *how, cow*; German: **Haus, raus, aufstehen**
- **ei** sounds like English *shy, mine*; German: **drei, zwei, Rhein, eins**
- **ie** sounds like English *here*; German: **vier, Tier, Bier**

Others

- ch: **after a, o** and **u** as in **Bach, doch** and **Tuch**: pronounced as in the Scottish word *loch*; after **e** and **i** as in **frech, dich**: pronounced like *h* in *huge*
- l, ll: **Halle, alle, Eltern** are prounounced much lighter than the English *l*
- sch: **Fisch, Busch** sound like *sh* in *short*
- w: **VW, wir, wann** sounds like *v* in *very*
- pronounce the *g* hard; **guten Tag, ganz genau**

Always pronounce the **e** at the end of a word: **Dose, Rose, Hose.** And always pronounce the **k** at the beginning of a word: **Kneipe, Kirsche, Kuh.**

The letter ß stands for 'ss'.

The same word but different pronunciation:

isolation	Isolation
depression	Depression
ambition	Ambition
progression	Progression
information	Information
blind	blind
butter	Butter
tiger	Tiger
tunnel	Tunnel
Berlin	Berlin
London	London

Capital letters

In German all nouns, names, cities, countries are written with a capital letter. You also write **Sie** (formal for *you*) and **Du** (informal) with capital letters when writing letters.

Dialects, idiomatic language, standard German and word building

There are three categories into which the German language can be divided. **Dialekt/Mundart** (*dialect*), **Umgangssprache** (*idiomatic language, local usage*) and **Hochdeutsch** (*High German/standard German*). **Hochdeutsch** is grammatically correct, free of accent and taught in all schools.

Umgangssprache is often just a few words and expressions of the city or area which are different. You can pick them up easily after a while.

There are, however, various dialects in Germany, Austria and Switzerland and local people speak this dialect. Among them are **Bayrisch, Hessisch, Sächsisch, Friesisch, Plattdeutsch, Schwäbisch** and, in Switzerland, **Schweitzerdeutsch**, which again changes from area to area (*Kanton*).

A dialect has its own words, the meaning of which might not be so clear to people speaking a different dialect.

So, use your Hochdeutsch. Everybody understands that.

Word building

Don't worry about long words. Try to spot familiar words within them. This also helps to build up your vocabulary.

Example: **Kinderlichtbildbescheinigung** = *passport for children*:

das Kind   *child*
die Kinder   *children*
das Licht   *the light*
das Bild   *the picture*
das Lichtbild   *photography*
die Bescheinigung   **certificate**
= **die Kinderlichtbildbescheinigung**

Use these types of expressions to build up your vocabulary and help to give structure to your sentences. Look out for word building examples throughout the book, too.

verstehen	*to understand*
das Verstehen	*understanding*
Ich verstehe Sie.	*I understand you.*
Ich verstehe Sie nicht.	*I don't understand you.*
Ich verstehe Sie, nicht ganz.	*I don't quite understand.*
Ich verstehe Sie, wenn Sie langsam sprechen.	*I understand when you speak slowly.*
Verstehen Sie mich?	*Do you understand me?*
Haben Sie mich verstanden?	*Did you understand me?*

Many English words and terms have been adopted into German, particularly computer technology (see Unit 3) and marketing jargon. The media, too, are using more and more

English expressions and words. Young people, in particular, use
English expressions and you will come across the following:

Das ist cool.	*That's cool.*
Mein Job gefällt mir gut.	*I like my job.*
Das war ein guter Joke.	*That was a good joke.*
Wir gehen morgen zu der Party.	*We are going to the party tomorrow.*
Das ist ein guter Song.	*That's a good song.*
Ich bin total happy.	*I am really happy.*
Hi!	*Hi!*
Du solltest mal wieder relaxen.	*You should relax again.*

Sorry!
Don't worry, be happy!

Verbs

relaxen	*to relax*
<u>ab</u>checken	*to check out*
<u>an</u>surfen	*to dial in, surf* (internet)
babysitten	*to do baby sitting*
downloaden	*to download*
mailen	*to send an email*
fighten	*to fight*
joggen	*to jog*
kidnappen	*to kidnap*
launchen	*to launch*
mergen	*to merge*
saven	*to save*

Nouns

der Actionfilm	Firstclass
aerobics	das Fitness center
die Beachparty	Lastminute-Flight
die Boxershorts	die Leggings
das Concert	der Lifestyle
der Computer	der Loser
der Export	die Lovestory
der Fanclub	der Nightclub
	das Poster

01

personal
matters

1.1 Titles, greetings and making arrangements

Core vocabulary

Titles

Mr	Herr
Mrs	Frau
Miss	Fräulein
Dr	Dr. Doktor/in
Prof.	Prof. Professor/in
Earl	Graf/Gräfin
Baron/ess	Baron/in

- **Fräulein** is an old-fashioned word and is hardly used any more. Most women prefer to be called **Frau** instead of **Fräulein** regardless of their marital status. **Fräulein** is only used to indicate the marital status.

- Addressing somebody with their title is important in Germany. If someone has a doctorial title (medical or academic) it is usual to address them as **Herr Doktor/Frau Doktor** with or without the surname: **Guten Tag, Herr Doktor, Guten Tag, Herr Doktor Meier, Guten Tag, Frau Doktor Meier.**

- At present both female and male titles can be used for female job titles, academic or medical professions: **Frau Rechtsanwältin** (+ surname), **Frau Rechtsanwalt** (+ surname). **Guten Tag, Frau Rechtsanwältin** (Meier), **Guten Tag, Frau Rechtsanwalt.**

Professor:	**Herr Professor** (+ surname), **Frau Professor/in** (+ surname).
Doctor (medical or academic):	**Herr Doktor, Frau Doktor/ Frau Doktorin.**
Judge:	**Herr Richter/Frau Richter/in.**
Mayor:	**Herr/Frau Bürgermeister/in.**
Member of parliament:	**Frau Abgeordnete/Herr Abgeordneter.**

When addressing nobility **Herr** or **Frau** is dropped: **Guten Tag Baronin Meier, Guten Tag Graf Meier.**

- Married people may have a double name (a combination of the two surnames). Use the whole name: **Guten Tag, Frau Meier-Hansen, Guten Tag, Herr Meier-Hansen.**

Greetings

The most common greetings are:

Hello	hallo
Good morning	guten Morgen
Good afternoon	guten Nachmittag
Good evening	guten Abend
Good night	gute Nacht
Goodbye	auf Wiedersehen
Goodbye (on the phone)	auf Wiederhören
Bye	tschüss

In southern Germany: **Grüß Gott** (*Greet God*). On the North Sea Coast and in Hamburg: **Moin, Moin** (*morning, morning*). In Switzerland: **Grützi** (*greet you*) and **Servus. Servus** can mean both *hello* and *bye*. **Tschau** (*cheerio*).

In Swabia, southern Germany: **Ade** (*bye*) and in Austria you'll hear **Auf Wiederschauen** and **Servus.**

Remember: A greeting that can be used throughout the day is **Guten Tag.**

Recent cultural changes: more and more young people and students just say **hi!**

Introducing someone

I would like to introduce you to …: **Ich möchte Ihnen gerne … vorstellen**

Mrs Meier	Frau Meier
Mr Meier	Herrn Meier
my husband/son	meinen Mann/Sohn
my wife/daughter	meine Frau/Tochter
my colleague	meinen Kollegen Herrn Meier
	meine Kollegin Frau Meier
	Herrn Professor Dr Schmidt
Are you Mrs …?	Sind Sie Frau …?
Mr …?	Sind Sie Herr …?
Mr Schmidt's (female) colleague?	Sind Sie die Kollegin von Herrn Schmidt?
Do you know each other?	Kennen Sie sich schon?
Pleased to meet you.	Freut mich Sie kennen zu lernen.

(Short form **freut mich** or **angenehm**)

Remember: Answer with **freut mich auch** or **angenehm.**

I am ...

single	ledig
married	verheiratet
divorced	geschieden
separated	getrennt
widowed	verwitwet
engaged	verlobt

Ich bin ...

Making arrangements

What shall we do this evening?	Was wollen wir heute Abend machen?
May I introduce myself?	Kann ich mich vorstellen?
This is (my wife/husband/ friend).	Das ist mein/e Frau/Mann Freund/Freundin.
Pleased to meet you.	Freut mich Sie kennen zu lernen.
May I sit here?	Kann ich hier sitzen? Kann ich hier Platz nehmen?
Are you alone?	Sind Sie alleine?
May I invite you to a ...?	Kann ich Sie zu ... einladen?
May I invite you for a coffee.	Kann ich Sie/dich zu einem Kaffee einladen.

bar	die Bar (s)
nightclub	der Nachtclub (s)
restaurant	das Restaurant (s)
theatre	das Theater (-)
cinema	das Kino (s)
disco	die Diskothek (en)
club	der Club (s)

drink	das Getränk (e)
meal	das Essen
dance	der Tanz (¨e)
show	die Show (s)
play	das Theaterstück (e)
musical	das Musical (s)
comedy	die Komödie (n)
concert	das Konzert (e)

What would you like to do?	Was möchten Sie gerne tun?
Where would you like to go?	Wohin möchten Sie gehen?
When shall we meet?	Wann sollen wir uns treffen?
I will pick you up.	Ich werde Sie abholen.
I don't mind.	Mir ist es gleich.
That's fine with me.	Das passt mir auch gut.

to *arrange a meeting*	ein Treffen vereinbaren
to *book a table*	einen Tisch buchen
to *go to the cinema*	ins Kino gehen
to *go to the theatre*	ins Theater gehen
to *go out*	<u>aus</u>gehen
to *go to a nightclub*	in einen Nachtclub gehen
to *watch a video*	ein Video <u>an</u>sehen

Useful phrases

Excuse me.	Entschuldigen Sie bitte/Entschuldige.
Pardon?	Entschuldigung? Wie bitte?
I don't understand.	Ich verstehe das nicht.
I did not catch that.	Ich habe das nicht ganz verstanden.
Can you speak more slowly?	Könnten Sie/kannst du etwas langsamer sprechen?
How do you say … in German?	Wie sagt man … auf Deutsch?
I apologize.	Entschuldigung.
I'm sorry.	Es tut mir Leid.
I beg your pardon.	Entschuldigung.
I didn't mean it.	Ich habe das nicht so gemeint.
Forgive me.	Verzeihung.
Sorry it was my fault.	Entschuldigung, das war mein Fehler.
It was your fault.	Es war Ihr/dein Fehler.
Thank you very much.	Vielen Dank/danke/danke schön/danke sehr.
I enjoyed it very much.	Ich habe es sehr genossen.
I had a lovely time.	Ich hatte eine wunderbare Zeit.
We must do it again sometime.	Wir sollten das irgendwann noch einmal machen.
I will see you again tomorrow.	Ich werde Sie/dich morgen <u>wieder</u>sehen.
I would like to see you again.	Ich würde Sie/dich gerne <u>wieder</u>sehen.
It's a pleasure.	Es freut mich.
Have good time!	Viel Spaß!
Have a safe journey.	Kommen Sie/komm gut nach Hause.

Good luck.	Viel Glück.
All the best.	Alles Gute.
Happy birthday!	Herzlichen Glückwunsch zum Geburtstag!
Merry Christmas!	Frohe Weihnachten!
Congratulations!	Herzlichen Glückwunsch!
Happy New Year!	Frohes Neues Jahr!
How are you?	Wie geht es Ihnen? Wie geht es Dir? Or wie geht's? (relatives, friends, young people among each other)
I am fine, thanks. And yourself?	Mir geht es gut, danke. Und Ihnen/dir/euch?
I am fine too.	Mir geht es auch gut.
very good	sehr gut
excellent	ausgezeichnet
I am not so well today.	Mir geht es nicht so gut heute.
I am a bit tired today.	Ich bin heute etwas müde.

i If you're stuck for something to say, try: **oh ja**, **ja ja**, **oh nein** or **ne**.

i In Germany you would expect a real answer to the question: 'Wie geht es Ihnen?' while in Britain the question is responded to with more of an echo.

Other expressions

see you soon	bis dann
see you later	bis später
have a nice weekend	schönes Wochenende
enjoy the rest of the day/evening	schönen Tag/Abend noch

Useful verbs

to introduce	sich <u>vor</u>stellen
to introduce somebody	jemanden <u>vor</u>stellen
to meet somebody	jemanden treffen
to get to know somebody	jemanden kennen lernen
to meet	treffen
to recognize	erkennen
to greet somebody	jemanden grüßen/begrüßen

Extras

die Begrüßung der Gäste	*welcoming of the guests*
die Vorstellung	*introduction* (can also mean *imagination* or *the performance*)
jemanden <u>vor</u>stellen	*to introduce somebody*
sich <u>vor</u>stellen	*to introduce* (or *imagine*)
stellen Sie sich bitte <u>vor</u>	*please introduce yourself*
das Treffen	*the meeting*
sich treffen	*to meet*
der Treffpunkt	*meeting place*
ein Treffen vereinbaren	*to arrange a meeting*
ein Treffen <u>ab</u>sagen	*to cancel a meeting*
zu einem Treffen erscheinen	*to turn up to a meeting*

Other meanings of the verb *sich vorstellen*

Stellen Sie sich <u>vor</u>, ich fliege auch nach Berlin.	*Guess what, I'm flying to Berlin too!*
Ich habe mir Ihren Bruder genauso <u>vor</u>gestellt.	*I imagined your brother exactly like that.*

Typical German expressions

Machen Sie es gut. (formal) Mach's gut. (informal)	*Have a good time.*
Viel Spaß!	*Have fun!*
Ich wünsche Ihnen eine gute Reise.	*Have a good journey.*
Mahlzeit!	*Bon appetit! (Have a good meal!)*
Viel Glück!	*Good luck!*
Gute Reise!	*Have a good journey!*
Gute Fahrt!	(used when people leave by car, bicycle etc.)
Herzlich willkommen!	*Come on in! Welcome!* (lit.: *heartily welcome!*)

1.2 Where are you from?

Core vocabulary

Where do you come from?   **Woher kommen Sie?**

I come from ...	Ich komme aus ...
I am ...	Ich bin ...
I speak ...	Ich spreche ...

I come from ...		*I am ...*	*I speak ...*
Austria	Österreich	Österreicher/in	österreichisch
Belgium	Belgien	Belgier/in	flämisch, französisch
England	England	Engländer/in	englisch
Finland	Finnland	Finne/in	finnisch
France	Frankreich	Franzose/in	französisch
Germany	Deutschland	Deutsche/r	deutsch
Greece	Griechenland	Grieche/in	griechisch
Ireland	Irland	Ire, Irin	irisch, gälisch, englisch
Italy	Italien	Italiener/in	italienisch
Scotland	Schottland	Schotte/in	schottisch
Spain	Spanien	Spanier/in	spanisch
Switzerland	die Schweiz	Schweizer/in	deutsch, französisch, italienisch
Turkey	die Türkei	Türke/in	türkisch
Wales	Wales	Waliser/in	walisisch
Bosnia	Bosnien	Bosnier/in	serbisch
Croatia	Kroatien	Kroate/in	kroatisch
Denmark	Dänemark	Däne/in	dänisch
Hungary	Ungarn	Ungar/in	ungarisch
Latvia	Lettland	Lette/Lettin	lettisch
Lithuania	Litauen	Litauer/in	litauisch
Norway	Norwegen	Norweger/in	norwegisch
Poland	Polen	Pole/in	polnisch
Romania	Rumänien	Rumäne/in	rumänisch
Russia	Russland	Russe/Russin	russisch
Sweden	Schweden	Schwede/in	schwedisch

Africa	Afrika	*India*	Indien
America	Amerika	*Iran*	Iran
Australia	Australien	*Iraq*	Irak
China	China	*New Zealand*	Neuseeland
Europe	Europa	*USA*	USA
Japan	Japan		

Useful phrases

Do you speak English?	Sprechen Sie Englisch?
Yes, I speak some English.	Ja, ich spreche etwas/ein wenig/ein bisschen Englisch.

What languages do you speak?	Welche Sprachen sprechen Sie?
I speak Spanish, German, Italian.	Ich spreche deutsch, spanisch, italienisch.
What nationality are you?	Was ist Ihre Nationalität/ Staatsangehörigkeit?
Where were you born?	Wo sind Sie geboren?
I was born in ...	Ich bin in ... geboren
I live in ...	Ich lebe/wohne in ...
in the north/south/east/west	im Norden, Süden, Osten, Westen
near the sea	in der Nähe vom Meer
on the coast	an der Küste
in the mountains	in den Bergen
in the city	in der Stadt
in a village	auf dem Dorf
in the suburbs	am Stadtrand
in the country	auf dem Land

Useful verbs

to live	leben	I live	ich lebe
to live	wohnen	I live	ich wohne
to speak	sprechen	I speak	ich spreche
to be born	geboren sein	I was born in ...	ich bin in ... geboren

Extras

Names of some cities and places which are different from English:

Athens	Athen	Hesse	Hessen
Baltic Sea	Ostsee	Lower Saxony	Niedersachsen
Bavaria	Bayern	North Sea	Nordsee
Bavarian Forest	Bayrischer Wald	Nuremberg	Nürnberg
Black Forest	Schwarzwald	Munich	München
Brussels	Brüssel	Moselle	Mosel
Brunswick	Braunschweig	Moscow	Moskau
Cologne	Köln	Rhine	Rhein
Lake Constance	Bodensee	Saxony	Sachsen
Hanover	Hannover	Thuringia	Thüringen

1.3 Personal appearance

Core vocabulary

Können Sie sich eventuell beschreiben?	*Could you perhaps describe yourself?*
Wie sehen Sie/siehst du aus?	*What are you like?*
Wie sieht er/sie aus?	*What does he/she look like?*
Er/sie ist ein/e …	*He/she is a …*

man	Mann	*woman*	Frau
girl	Mädchen	*boy*	Junge
teenager	Teenager	*child*	Kind
baby	Baby	*adult*	Erwachsener
youth	Jugendlicher		

Use the following grid to describe yourself and someone you know well:

I am ich bin	*quite* relativ	*tall* groß
Are you ... Sind Sie	*very* sehr	*small* klein?
He/She is Er/sie ist	*average* durchschnittlich	*tall* groß

I am Ich bin	*quite*	relativ	*tall*	groß
	very	sehr	*small*	klein
	rather	eher	*slim*	dünn
	average	durchschnittlich	*well built*	vollschlank
			tall	groß

I have ich habe	*long* lange	*blonde hair* blonde Haare
He has er hat	*short* kurze	*brown hair* braune Haare
She has sie hat	*medium length* mittellange	*dark hair* dunkle Haare
I have Ich habe	*blue*, brown** blaue, braune *green** grüne	*eyes* Augen

*For more colours see page 35.

looks	das Aussehen
to look like	<u>aus</u>sehen
I look …	Ich sehe … <u>aus</u>.
he looks attractive	er sieht attraktiv <u>aus</u>
person, character	der Typ

He is a great person.		Er ist ein super Typ.	
He seems to be well balanced.		Er scheint ausgeglichen zu sein.	
He seems to be very friendly.		Er scheint sehr freundlich zu sein.	
He seems to be very balanced.		Er wirkt sehr ausgeglichen.	
likeable		sympathisch	

person, character — die Person, der Charakter

She is an extremely likeable/unlikeable person. — Sie ist eine ausgesprochen sympathische/unsympathische Person.

The woman looks really cool. — Die Frau sieht total cool <u>aus</u>.

She has a strong/weak personality. — Sie ist eine starke/schwache Persönlichkeit.

He is good looking. — Er ist gut aussehend.

attractive	attraktiv	unattractive	unattraktiv
fashionable	modisch	unfashionable	altmodisch
interesting	interessant	uninteresting	uninteressant
fit	sportlich	unfit	unsportlich
good looking	gut aussehend	ugly	hässlich
neat	gepflegt	untidy	ungepflegt
smart	schick	scruffy	herunter-gekommen
ordinary	gewöhnlich	different	ungewöhnlich
tall	groß	short	klein
underweight	untergewichtig	overweight	übergewichtig
well built	vollschlank	slim	schlank
anorexic	magersüchtig	obese	fettleibig
right handed	Rechtshänder	left handed	Linkshänder
short sighted	kurzsichtig	long sighted	weitsichtig
agoraphobic	agoraphobisch	claustrophobic	klaustro-phobisch

Useful phrases

How much do you weigh?	Wie viel wiegen Sie/wiegst du?
I weigh 75 kg.	Ich wiege 75 kg.
How tall are you?	Wie groß sind Sie/bist du?
I am 1.59m.	Ich bin 1,59 (Meter).

Useful verbs

to look like someone	wie jemand <u>aus</u>sehen
I look like …	Ich sehe <u>aus</u> wie …
to put on weight	<u>zu</u>nehmen
I am putting on weight	Ich nehme <u>zu</u>
to lose weight	<u>ab</u>nehmen
I am losing weight	Ich nehme <u>ab</u>
to get fit	fit werden
I am getting fit	Ich werde fit

Extras

Er/sie ist	*He/she is*
in der Pubertät	*in puberty*
im Teenager-Alter	*in his/her teens*
im Jugendalter	*an adolescence*
Mitte zwanzig	*mid-twenty*
mittleren Alters	*middle aged*
in der Midlifecrisis	*having a midlife crisis*
in den Wechseljahren	*in the menopause*
in einem gewissen Alter	*of a certain age*
im hohen Alter	*old age*
im Rentenalter	*age of retirement*

1.4 What sort of person are you?

Core vocabulary

I am Ich bin	*shy/talkative* schüchtern/redselig
Are you Sind Sie/bist du	*happy/unhappy* glücklich/ unglücklich?
He is Er ist	*friendly/unfriendly* freundlich/ unfreundlich
She is Sie ist	*good/helpful* gut/hilfsbereit

Character and feelings

hard working	fleißig	*lazy*	faul
interesting	interessant	*uninteresting*	uninteressant
nice	nett	*nasty*	böse
quiet	ruhig	*loud*	laut
reliable	zuverlässig	*unreliable*	unzuverlässig
funny	lustig	*serious*	ernst
crazy, mad	verrückt	*boring*	langweilig
strange, odd	merkwürdig	*normal*	normal
considerate	rücksichtsvoll	*inconsiderate*	rücksichtslos
capable	fähig	*useless*	unfähig
confident	selbstbewusst	*nervous*	nervös
generous	großzügig	*mean*	geizig
helpful	hilfsbereit	*unhelpful*	nicht hilfsbereit
odd	merkwürdig	*normal*	normal
polite	höflich	*rude*	unhöflich
practical	praktisch	*impractical*	unpraktisch
reliable	zuverlässig	*unreliable*	unzuverlässig
relaxed	entspannt	*uptight*	angespannt
sensitive	sensibel	*unfeeling*	unsensibel
serious	ernst	*frivolous*	leichtsinnig
sincere	aufrichtig	*insincere*	unaufrichtig
strong willed	willensstark	*weak*	willensschwach
reserved	verschlossen	*receptive*	aufgeschlossen
stubborn	stur	*open minded*	aufgeschlossen
courageous	mutig	*frightened*	furchtsam

The five senses

sight	das Sehvermögen	*to see*	sehen	*I see*	ich sehe
hearing	das Gehör	*to hear*	hören	*I hear*	ich höre
taste	der Geschmack	*to taste*	schmecken	*I taste*	ich schmecke
smell	der Geruch	*to smell*	riechen	*I smell*	ich rieche
touch	das Gefühl	*to touch*	fühlen	*I touch*	ich fühle

Useful phrases

He/she has ...	Er/Sie hat ...
a sense of humour	einen Sinn für Humor

plenty of willpower	eine starke Willenskraft
a kind heart	ein offenes Herz
a weakness for	eine Schwäche für
a good imagination	eine gute Vorstellungskraft

Useful verbs

to be bored	gelangweilt sein
I am bored	ich bin gelangweilt
to be interested in ...	sich interessieren für ...
I am interested in ...	ich interessiere mich für ...
to be worried about ...	sich Sorgen machen um/wegen ...
I am worried	Ich mache mir Sorgen um/wegen

Extras

besorgt sein um	*to be worried about*
Angst haben vor	*to be scared of*
eine Schwäche haben für	*to have a weakness for*
eine Sympathie haben für	*to feel an affection for*

1.5 My things

Core vocabulary

bag	die Tasche (n)
briefcase	die Aktentasche (n)
cheque book	das Scheckbuch (¨er)
credit card	die Kreditkarte (n)
diary	der Terminkalender (-)
driving licence	der Führerschein (e)
glasses/sunglasses	die Brille/die Sonnenbrille (n)
keys	die Schlüssel
notebook	der Notizblock (¨e)
notepaper	das Briefpapier (-)
passport	der Personalausweis (e)
pencil	der Bleistift (e)
purse	der Geldbeutel (-)
wallet	die Brieftasche (n)
watch	die Uhr (en)

The word for *your*, *his* and *her* usually follows the same pattern as the word for *my*. See page 14 in the toolbox.

On my desk: my ...

computer	mein Computer
disk	meine Diskette
fax machine	mein Fax
hard drive	meine Festplatte
mobile	mein Handy
mouse	meine Maus
laptop	mein Laptop
palmtop	mein Palm
phone	mein Telefon
printer	mein Drucker
scanner	mein Scanner

At home: my ...

DVD	mein DVD-Spieler
CD player	mein CD-Spieler
discs	meine Disketten
camera	meine Kamera, mein Fotoapparat
video camera	meine Videokamera
digital camera	meine Digitalekamera
film	mein Film
photos	meine Fotos

My friends

girlfriend (f)	meine Freundin
boyfriend (m)	mein Freund
girlfriends	meine Freundinnen
boyfriends	meine Freunde
colleagues	meine Kollegen
boss	mein Chef
university colleague	mein Studienfreund

Here are a few expressions used in colloquial German:

all my stuff	mein ganzes Zeug
all my papers	meine ganzen Unterlagen
my bumf	mein Papierkram
all this stuff	der ganze Kram
all this junk	das ganze Gerümpel
bookcase	das Bücherregal

Useful phrases

Have you got a ...?	Haben Sie ein/e/en ...?
I have lost my ...	Ich habe mein/e/n ... verloren
I can't find my ...	Ich kann mein/e/n ... nicht finden
Have you seen my ...?	Haben Sie/Hast du mein/e/n ... gesehen?

Useful verbs

to email	mailen
to find	finden
to forget	vergessen
to fax	faxen
to lose/mislay	verlieren/verlegen
to print out	<u>aus</u>drucken
to reduce	verkleinern
to enlarge	vergrößern

1.6 I think, I feel

Useful compound words

to like	mögen	*liking*	die Zuneigung	*I like*	ich mag
to love	lieben	*love*	die Liebe	*I love*	ich liebe
to prefer	<u>vor</u>ziehen	*preference*	die Vorliebe	*I prefer*	ich ziehe <u>vor</u>
to dislike	nicht mögen	*dislike*	die Abneigung	*I dislike*	ich mag ... nicht
to hate	hassen	*hate*	der Hass	*I hate*	ich hasse

Core vocabulary

To indicate that you like something or like doing something, you use **mögen** and **gerne**. Use **mögen** in connection with a noun:

I like pizza	Ich mag Pizza
I like jazz music	Ich mag Jazzmusik
We like sport	Wir mögen Sport
He liked the film	Er hat den Film gemocht
They liked our presentation	Sie mochten unseren Vortrag

The verb **mögen**: ich mag, du magst, er/sie/es mag, wir mögen, ihr mögt, sie mögen, Sie mögen.

To say *to like doing something*, you use **etwas gerne tun**. Simply add **gerne** and the *verb* to indicate that you like doing it:

I dance	ich tanze
I like dancing	ich tanze **gerne**
I like reading	ich lese **gerne**
she likes studying	sie studiert **gerne**
he liked talking	er hat **gerne** geredet
we liked to dance	wir haben **gerne** getanzt
she liked jogging	sie joggte **gerne**

i In German **lieben** is used more in connection with a person and not so much for things. You use **mögen** for things, **lieben** for people.

to love, **lieben**: *I love*, **ich liebe**; *love*, **die Liebe**; *to love*, **sich lieben**; *to make love*, **Liebe machen/sich lieben**:

I love my house.	I mag mein Haus.
I love my children.	Ich liebe meine Kinder.
They made love.	Sie machten Liebe/Sie liebten sich.

There are also two ways of expressing *to prefer*: you can use either **vorziehen** or **etwas lieber tun**: **lieber** in connection with a verb:

Ich gehe lieber.	*I prefer to walk.*
Ich fahre lieber.	*I prefer to drive.*

You can also use **lieber** in connection with a noun:

Ich höre lieber klassische Musik.	*I prefer listening to classical music.*
Sie geht lieber in die Oper.	*She prefers going to the opera.*

Remember: <u>vor</u>ziehen is more formal than **lieber**. It a separable verb:

Ich ziehe Tennis <u>vor</u>.	*I prefer tennis.*
Er zieht es <u>vor</u> alleine zu gehen.	*He prefers to go on his own.*
Ziehen Sie es <u>vor</u>, den Zug zu nehmen?	*Do you prefer taking the train?*

to dislike	nicht mögen
I don't like that.	Ich mag das nicht.
She does not like to fly.	Sie fliegt nicht gerne.

to hate	hassen
You should not hate him.	Sie sollten ihn nicht hassen.
I don't hate anything.	Ich hasse nichts.
Do you hate the rain?	Hassen Sie den Regen?

to believe	glauben	belief	der Glaube	I believe	ich glaube
to feel	fühlen	feeling	das Gefühl	I feel	ich fühle
to think	denken	thought	der Gedanke	I think	ich denke
to worry	sich sorgen	worry	die Sorge	I worry	ich sorge mich
to advise somebody	jemandem raten	advice	der Rat	I advise you	Ich rate Ihnen/dir
to encourage	ermutigen	encouragement	die Ermutigung	I encourage you	ich ermutige Sie/dich
to exaggerate	übertreiben	exaggeration	die Übertreibung	I am exaggerating	ich übertreibe
to joke	einen Witz machen	joke	der Witz	I am joking	ich mache einen Witz
to lie	lügen	lie	die Lüge	I am lying	ich lüge
to promise	versprechen	promise	das Versprechen	I promise	ich verspreche

Verbs taking dative or accusative

A small number of verbs are followed by the dative. The best approach here is to memorize them. Here are some common examples.

Verbs which take the dative

glauben (*to believe*)
ich glaube ihm/ihr — *I believe him/her*
danken (*to thank*)
Ich danke ihm für die Blumen. — *I thank him for the flowers.*
gefallen (*to please*)
Das Kleid gefällt mir. — *I like the dress* (lit. *The dress pleases me*).
vertrauen (*to trust*)
Ich vertraue ihm/ihr. — *I trust him/her.*

Other examples of verbs taking the dative

jemandem etwas raten (*to advise*) Ich rate ihm/ihr mehr Sport zu treiben *I advise him/her to do more sport.*

jemandem etwas versprechen (*to promise*) Ich verspreche meiner Sekretärin eine Gehaltserhöhung. *I promise my secretary a pay rise.*

Verbs which take the accusative

Many reflexive verbs are followed by the accusative, because the pronoun is the direct object:

sich waschen (*to wash*) Ich wasche mich. *I wash myself.*

sich <u>hin</u>setzen (*to sit down*) Kann ich mich hier <u>hin</u>setzen? *Can I sit down here?*

sich verlaufen (*to get lost*) Ich habe mich verlaufen. *I got lost.*

sich <u>um</u>ziehen (*to get changed*) Sie zieht sich <u>um</u>. *She gets changed.*

sich freuen auf (*to look forward to*) Ich freue mich auf mein Essen. *I am looking forward to my food.*

sich verlassen auf (*to rely on*) Ich kann mich auf ihn verlassen. *I can rely on him.*

Other examples of verbs taking the accusative

<u>an</u>rufen (*to phone*) Ich rufe dich <u>an</u>. *I phone you.*

fotografieren (*to take pictures*) Ich fotografiere meine Tante. *I take a picture of my aunt.*

<u>ab</u>holen (*to collect*) Ich hole Sie am Bahnhof <u>ab</u>. *I collect you at the train station.*

<u>wieder</u>sehen (*to see again*) Ich sehe dich bald <u>wieder</u>. *I'll see you again soon.*

besuchen (*to visit*) Ich besuche meinen Enkel in Berlin. *I visit my grandson in Berlin.*

<u>ein</u>laden (*to invite*) Ich lade Sie gerne zu einem Kaffee <u>ein</u>. *I would like to invite you for a coffee.*

suchen (*to look for*) Ich suche die Hauptstraße. *I am looking for the Hauptstrasse.*

jemanden mögen (*to like somebody/something*) Ich mag ihn. *I like him.*

jemanden lieben (*to love somebody/something*) Ich liebe sie. *I love her.*

jemanden <u>vor</u>ziehen (*to prefer somebody/something*) Ich ziehe ihn <u>vor</u>. *I prefer him.*

an jemanden denken (*to think about somebody/something*) Ich denke an ihn. *I am thinking about him.*

sich Sorgen machen über (*to worry about somebody/something*) Ich mache mir Sorgen über meinen Vater. *I am worried about my father.*

jemanden ermutigen (*to encourage somebody*) Ich ermutige meinen Sohn mit dem Rauchen <u>aufzuhören</u>. *I encourage my son to stop smoking.*

Witze machen über (*to make jokes about something/ somebody*) Ich mache einen Witz über Politiker. *I am making a joke about politicians.*

hassen (*to hate*) Ich hasse es. *I hate it.*

Examples of verbs and prepositions taking the accusative

denken **an** *to think about* Ich denke an dich. *I'm thinking about you.*

erinnern **an** *to remind* Du erinnerst mich an deine Schwester. *You remind me of your sister.*

glauben **an** *to believe in* Ich glaube an den Frieden. *I believe in peace.*

stolz sein **auf** *to be proud of* Ich bin stolz auf dich. *I am proud of you.*

sich freuen **auf** *to look forward to* Ich freue mich auf unseren Urlaub. *I am looking forward to our holiday.*

sich bedanken **für** *to thank for* Ich bedanke mich für den Brief. *I thank you for the letter.*

sich interessieren **für** *to be interested in* Ich interessiere mich für moderne Kunst. *I am interested in modern art.*

Examples of verbs with prepositions taking the dative

beginnen **mit** *to start with* Ich beginne mit meinem Reitunterricht. *I'm starting my horse riding classes.*

<u>auf</u>hören **mit** *to stop with* Ich höre mit dem Rauchen <u>auf</u>. *I stop smoking.*

träumen **von** *to dream of* Ich träume von ihm. *I dream of him.*

sich erholen **von** *to recover from* Ich erhole mich von meiner Operation. *I recover from my operation.*

enttäuscht sein **von** (*to be disappointed*) Ich bin von ihr/ihm enttäuscht. *I am disappointed in her/him.*

überzeugt sein **von** (*to be convinced/to be sure of*) Sie ist sehr von sich überzeugt. *She is very sure of herself.*

Prepositions taking the dative or accusative

dative = no motion   accusative = motion

an *at* **An dem** Strand ist es schön. *It is nice on the beach.* (no motion)
Ich gehe **an den** Strand. *I go to the beach.* (motion)

in *in* Ich studiere **in der** Schule. *I study at school.*
Ich gehe **in die** Schule. *I go to school.*

auf *on* Ich lege das Buch **auf den** Tisch. *I put the book on the table.*
Auf dem Tisch liegt ein Buch. *There is a book on the table.*

hinter *behind* Ich fahre das Fahrrad **hinter den** Garten. *I drive the bike behind the garden.*
Das Fahrrad ist **hinter dem** Garten. *The bike is behind the garden.*

neben *next to* Er fährt das Auto **neben das** Haus. *He drives the car beside the house.*
Das Auto steht **neben dem** Haus. *The car is parked beside the house.*

über *over* Das Flugzeug fliegt **über die** Insel. *The plane is flying over the island.*
Dicke Wolken sind **über der** Insel. *Over the island are heavy clouds.*

Negative and positive experiences

to be disappointed	enttäuscht sein	*I am disappointed*	ich bin enttäuscht
to be relieved	erleichtert sein	*I am relieved*	ich bin erleichtert
to be depressed	deprimiert sein	*I am depressed*	ich bin deprimiert
to be elated	begeistert sein	*I am elated*	ich bin begeistert
to be stressed	gestresst sein	*I am stressed*	ich bin gestresst
to be relaxed	relaxed sein	*I am relaxed*	ich bin relaxed
to be discouraged	entmutigt sein	*I am discouraged*	ich bin entmutigt
to be encouraged	ermutigt sein	*I am encouraged*	ich bin ermutigt
to be nervous	nervös sein	*I am nervous*	ich bin nervös
to be confident	zuversichtlich sein	*I am confident*	ich bin zuversichtlich
to be worried	sich Sorgen machen	*I am worried*	ich mache mir Sorgen
to be reassured	beruhigt sein	*I am reassured*	ich bin beruhigt
to be sad	traurig sein	*I am sad*	ich bin traurig
to be happy	fröhlich	*I am happy*	ich bin fröhlich
to be ashamed	sich schämen	*I am ashamed*	ich schäme mich
to be proud	stolz sein	*I am proud*	ich bin stolz
to be unfortunate	Pech haben	*I am unfortunate*	ich habe Pech
to be lucky	Glück haben	*I am lucky*	ich habe Glück

Verbs which are used with another verb

(would like to)	*(möchten)*	*I would like to go to the market-place.*	Ich möchte zum Marktplatz gehen.
to have to	müssen	*I must leave.*	Ich muss gehen.
to be allowed to	dürfen	*You are not allowed to smoke here.*	Sie dürfen hier nicht rauchen.
ought to	sollen	*I ought to stay at home.*	Ich sollte zu Hause bleiben.

Useful compound words

lieben *to love*	lieb gewinnen *to grow fond of*	lieb haben *to be fond of*
liebevoll *loving*	lieblos *unloving*	liebenswert *loveable*
lieblich *lovely*	liebenswürdigerweise *kindly*	die Liebenswürdigkeit *politeness*
der Gedanke *the thought*	die Gedankenlosigkeit *absent-mindedness*	gedankenlos *absent minded*
gedankenvoll *thoughtful*	die Gedankenarmut *lack of thought*	gedanklich *intellectual/imaginary*
der bloße Gedanke an *the mere thought of*	etwas in Gedanken tun *to do something distractedly*	
der Mut *the courage*	den Mut verlieren *to lose courage/heart*	wieder Mut bekommen *to gain confidence*
mutig sein *to be courageous*	mutlos *discouraged*	
die Mutlosigkeit *discouragement*	die Ermutigung *encouragement*	ermutigen *to encourage*
die Entmutigung *discouragement*	entmutigen *to discourage*	

1.7 Expressing an opinion

Useful verbs and phrases

to believe glauben   *I believe* ich glaube
to consider something etwas in Betracht ziehen   *I consider* ich ziehe … in Betracht
to think denken   *I think* ich denke
to express <u>aus</u>drücken   *I express* ich drücke … <u>aus</u>
to agree <u>zu</u>stimmmen   *I agree* ich stimme … <u>zu</u>   *I agree with you.* Ich stimme Ihnen/dir <u>zu</u>.
disagree nicht <u>zu</u>stimmen   *I don't agree* Ich stimme … nicht <u>zu</u>
I don't agree with you. Ich stimme Ihnen/dir nicht <u>zu</u>.
to argue argumentieren   *I argue* Ich argumentiere   *I argue with my brother.*   Ich argumentiere mit meinem Bruder
to discuss bereden   *I discuss* ich berede
to ask fragen   *I ask* ich frage   *I would like to ask you something.* Ich möchte Sie/dich etwas fragen.
to dispute sich streiten   *I dispute* ich streite mich
to question in Frage stellen   *I question* Ich stelle … in Frage
I question what you are saying. Ich stelle was Sie sagen/du sagst in Frage.
to quote zitieren   *I quote* ich zitiere
to request bitten   *I request* ich bitte   *I would like to request something.* Ich möchte Sie/dich um etwas bitten.
to suggest <u>vor</u>schlagen   *I suggest* ich schlage <u>vor</u>
to compare vergleichen   *I compare* ich vergleiche
to differ unterscheiden   *I differ* ich unterscheide
to discuss diskutieren   *I discuss* ich diskutiere
to conclude zum Schluss kommen   *I conclude* Ich komme zum Schluss

Ich glaube, dass man mehr für die Umwelt tun sollte. *I believe that we should do more for the environment.*
Ich stimme Ihnen total <u>zu</u>. *I agree with you completely.*

Das ist völliger Unsinn. *That is complete nonsense.*

on the one hand	einerseits
on the other hand	andererseits
first	erstens
second	zweitens
finally	schließlich

actually	eigentlich
basically	grundsätzlich
clearly	klar
consequently	folglich
fortunately/unfortunately	glücklicherweise/ unglücklicherweise
generally	im Allgemeinen
honestly	ehrlich
mainly	hauptsächlich
normally	normalerweise
obviously	offensichtlich
particularly	besonders/vor allem
principally	prinzipiell
really	wirklich
usually/unusually	gewöhnlich/ungewöhnlich
in my/his/her opinion	meiner/seiner/ihrer Meinung nach
above all	vor allem/vor allen Dingen
although	obwohl
as a result	als Ergebnis
as well as	sowohl … als auch …
however	jedoch
in many respects	in vielen Punkten
in spite of	trotz
instead of	anstelle
nevertheless	desto trotz
otherwise	andererseits
similarly	ähnlich
the reason is …	der Grund dafür ist …
to tell the truth	um die Wahrheit zu sagen
I wish I could agree	ich wünschte ich könnte zustimmen
I beg to differ	ich bin anderer Ansicht
I mean	ich meine
I maintain	ich behaupte
for example	zum Beispiel
etc.	usw/und so weiter
in brief	kurz dargestellt
the advantages/disadvantages are …	die Vorteile/Nachteile sind …
the pros and cons	Pro und Kontra

the pro and cons	Für und Wider
to conclude	zum Ergebnis kommen
it is	es ist
bad/good	schlecht/gut
complicated/easy	kompliziert/einfach
better/worse	besser/schlechter
nice/not very nice	schön/nicht sehr schön
too hard/easy	zu schwer/leicht
subjective	subjektiv
objective	objektiv
it is not	es ist nicht
objective	objektiv
realistic	realistisch
logical	logisch
It does not make any sense.	Es macht keinen Sinn.
It does not change what you say.	Das ändert nicht was Sie/du sagen/sagst.

That is completely incorrect. Das ist völlig falsch.
The argument does not convince me. Das Argument überzeugt mich nicht.
That is nonsense. Das ist Unsinn/Quatsch.
Why do you say that? Warum sagen Sie das?
You have to explain that more precisely. Sie müssen das genauer erklären.

der Streit *the argument/the fight* sich streiten *to argue, to quarrel, to squabble, to fight, to take legal action* Die Kinder streiten sich den ganzen Tag. *The children argue the whole day.* streitsüchtig *quarrelsome* Sie sind richtig streitsüchtig. *They are really quarrelsome.* die Streiterei *quarrelling* der Streithahn *squabbler* Du bist ein richtiger Streithahn. *You are a real squabbler*

der Fall *the case* im Streitfall *in case of dispute* im Streitfall Klein gegen Braun *in the case of Klein versus Braun* Sie bekamen Streit wegen dem Abfall. *They argued about the rubbish.* Hört/Hören Sie mit dem Streit auf! *Stop arguing!*

1.8 I do (I + useful action verbs)

Useful verbs

to wake up	aufwachen	I wake up	ich wache auf
to get up	aufstehen	I get up	ich stehe auf
to take a shower	duschen	I take a shower	ich dusche
to get dressed	sich anziehen	I get dressed	ich ziehe mich an
to eat	essen	I eat	ich esse
to drink	trinken	I drink	ich trinke
to work	arbeiten	I work	ich arbeite
to go to work	zur Arbeit fahren	I go to work	ich fahre zur Arbeit
to start work	anfangen zu arbeiten	I start work	ich fange an zu arbeiten
to stop work	aufhören zu arbeiten	I stop work	ich höre auf zu arbeiten
to interrupt work	die Arbeit unterbrechen	I interrupt my work	ich unterbreche meine Arbeit
to take a break	eine Pause machen	I take a break	ich mache eine Pause
to go for a break	zur Pause gehen	I go for a break	ich gehe zur Pause
to go home	nach Hause gehen	I go home	ich gehe nach Hause
to play	spielen	I play	ich spiele
to watch television	fernsehen	I watch television	ich gucke/ sehe fern
to read	lesen	I read	ich lese
to get washed	sich waschen	I get washed	ich wasche mich
to go to bed	ins Bett gehen	I go to bed	ich gehe ins Bett
to laugh	lachen	I laugh	ich lache
to smile	lächeln	I smile	ich lächele
to giggle	kichern	I giggle	ich kichere
to sleep	schlafen	I sleep	ich schlafe
to dream	träumen	I dream	ich träume
to rush	sich beeilen	I am in a rush	ich muss mich beeilen
to relax	sich ausruhen	I relax	ich ruhe mich aus/ich relaxe

Coming and going verbs

All these verbs take **sein** in the perfect tense.

to walk	gehen	I walk	ich gehe
to go for a walk	spazieren gehen	I go for a walk	ich gehe spazieren
to run	rennen	I run	ich renne
to ride a bicycle	Fahrrad fahren	I ride a bicycle	ich fahre Fahrrad
to drive	fahren	I drive	ich fahre
to arrive	<u>an</u>kommen	I depart	ich fahre <u>ab</u>
to enter	<u>ein</u>treten	I leave	ich gehe <u>raus</u>
to come	kommen	I go	ich gehe
to go up	<u>hoch</u>gehen	I go down	ich gehe <u>runter</u>
to stay	bleiben	I return	ich kehre <u>zurück</u>

Communicating

to speak	sprechen
to repeat something	etwas wiederholen
to talk to someone	mit jemandem sprechen
to whisper to someone	jemandem etwas <u>zu</u>flüstern
to shout at someone	jemanden <u>an</u>schreien
to ask a question	eine Frage stellen
to phone	telefonieren
to ask for something	nach etwas fragen
to respond to a question	eine Frage beantworten
to tell a story	eine Geschichte erzählen
to enjoy yourself	sich amüsieren
to be angry	ärgerlich sein
to have trouble/difficulty	Schwierigkeiten haben
to get depressed	deprimiert sein
to know someone	jemanden kennen
to know something	etwas wissen
to cheat	schummeln
to trick	hereinlegen, übers Ohr legen
to challenge	herausfordern
to compliment	jemandem ein Kompliment machen
to neglect	vernachlässigen

Useful verbs

<u>ein</u>steigen	<u>aus</u>steigen	to get in/get out
<u>rein</u>kommen	<u>raus</u>kommen	to enter/to leave
<u>hoch</u>gehen	<u>runter</u>gehen	to walk up/to walk down

<u>runter</u>kommen	<u>rauf</u>kommen	*to come down/to come up*
<u>weg</u>gehen	<u>hin</u>gehen	*to leave/to go to*
<u>weg</u>fahren	<u>hin</u>fahren	*to drive away/to drive to*
<u>ein</u>schlafen	<u>aus</u>schlafen	*to fall asleep/to sleep in/ have a lie-in*
<u>an</u>schreien	<u>auf</u>schreien	*to shout at/to shout out*

feiern *to celebrate* die Feier *the celebration*
der Feierabend *end of work* Schönen Feierabend! *Enjoy your evening off work!*

1.9 Don't panic!

Calm down!	Beruhigen Sie sich! /Beruhige dich!
Help!	Hilfe!
Be careful!	<u>Auf</u>passen!
Careful!	Vorsicht!
Watch out!	Achtung!
Stay back!	<u>Zurück</u>bleiben!
Down!	Runter!
Listen!	Hören Sie/Hör <u>zu</u>!
I said no.	Ich sagte nein.
No, thanks.	Nein, danke.
It is enough.	Es ist genug.
Be careful!	Pass <u>auf</u>!/Passen Sie <u>auf</u>!
Do you understand me?	Verstehen Sie mich? Verstehst du mich?
Can you help me?	Können Sie mir helfen?
Do you speak English?	Sprechen Sie/Sprichst du Englisch?
Can you say it again more slowly?	Können Sie/Kannst du das noch mal langsam sagen?
I didn't catch what you said.	Ich habe das nicht <u>mit</u>gekriegt.
Do you understand?	Verstehen Sie?/Verstehst Du?
Please can you find someone who speaks English?	Können Sie/Kannst du jemanden finden der Englisch spricht?
Can you write it down for me, please?	Können Sie/Kannst du es bitte für mich <u>auf</u>schreiben?
How do you spell it?	Wie buchstabieren Sie/ buchstabierst du das?
Have you got the phone number for ...?	Haben Sie/hast du die Telefonnummer für ...?

What do I need to dial first?   Was muss ich zuerst wählen?
What is the code for ...?   Wie ist die Vorwahl für ...?
How do I get an outside line?   Wie bekomme ich ein
                 Außenamt?

i Some useful signs

Feuerwehreinfahrt	*Fire brigade entrance*
Notfallaufnahme	*Emergency entrance*
Achtung!	*Danger!*
<u>Auf</u>passen!	*Watch out!*
Warnung!	*Warning!*
Vorsicht!	*Careful!*
Kein Eingang	*No entrance*

02

family

2.1 My family

Core vocabulary

my family and relatives	meine Familie und Verwandten
my mother	meine Mutter
my father	mein Vater
my parents	meine Eltern
my sister	meine Schwester
my brother	mein Bruder
my step-brother	mein Stiefbruder
my step-sister	meine Stiefschwester
my twin brother	mein Zwillingsbruder
my twin sister	meine Zwillingsschwester
my grandmother	meine Großmutter
my grandfather	mein Großvater
my grandparents	meine Großeltern
my uncle	mein Onkel
my aunt	meine Tante
my cousin	mein Cousin/meine Cousine
great-grandparents	meine Urgroßeltern

This is ... *Das ist ...*

my husband	mein Mann
my wife	meine Frau
my father-in-law	mein Schwiegervater
my mother-in-law	meine Schwiegermutter
my brother-in-law	mein Schwager
my sister-in-law	meine Schwägerin
my younger brother	mein jüngerer Bruder
my younger sister	meine jüngere Schwester
my older brother	mein älterer Bruder
my older sister	meine ältere Schwester
my grandson	mein Enkelsohn
my granddaughter	meine Enkeltochter
my partner	mein Partner/meine Partnerin
my friend	mein Freund/meine Freundin
my boyfriend	mein Freund
my girlfriend	meine Freundin
my godson	mein Patensohn
my goddaughter	meine Patentochter
my nephew	mein Neffe
my niece	meine Nichte

a married couple	ein verheiratetes Paar
widow	eine Witwe
widower	ein Witwer
family planning/contraception	die Familienplanung/ Verhütung
condom	das Kondom
the pill	die Pille
the coil	die Spirale
the morning-after pill	die Pille danach
vasectomy	die Sterilisation

May I introduce my ... *Darf ich ... <u>vor</u>stellen*

Pleased to meet you	freut mich Sie/dich kennen zu lernen
I am sorry to hear about your separation/divorce.	Ich habe von Ihrer Trennung/ Scheidung/gehört; das tut mir Leid.
Will you go out with me?	Möchten Sie/möchtest du mit mir <u>aus</u>gehen?
I am going out with ...	Ich gehe <u>aus</u> mit ...
We are just good friends.	Wir sind nur gute Freunde.

Useful verbs

to like someone	jemanden mögen	*I like*	ich mag
to flirt	flirten	*I flirt*	ich flirte
to kiss	küssen	*I kiss*	ich küsse
to go out with someone	mit jemandem <u>aus</u>gehen		
I'm going out with ...	Ich gehe mit ... <u>aus</u>		
to get on with someone	sich gut verstehen mit		
I get on well with ...	Ich verstehe mich gut mit ...		
to have a good time	sich amüsieren		
I'm having a good time	Ich amüsiere mich		
to have intercourse/sex	Geschlechtsverkehr haben/Sex haben		
I'm sleeping with ...	Ich habe Sex mit/ich schlafe mit ...		
to get married	heiraten		
I'm getting married	ich heirate		
to get on each other's nerves	sich auf die Nerven gehen		
He gets on my nerves.	Er geht mir auf die Nerven.		
to look after someone	sich um jemanden kümmern		
I'm looking after ...	Ich kümmere mich um ...		

to quarrel	sich streiten	I'm quarrelling	ich streite mich...
to separate	sich trennen	I'm separating from ...	ich trenne mich von ...
to divorce	sich scheiden lassen	I'm getting divorced.	Ich lasse mich scheiden.
to fall in love	sich verlieben	I'm in love.	Ich bin verliebt.

Pet names

der Kosename	*pet name*
Liebling	*darling*
Herzchen	*sweetheart*
Süße/r	*honey*
Schatz	*sweetheart*
Schätzchen	*little sweetheart*
Engelchen	*little angel*
Omi	*granny*
Opi	*grandpa*
Mami	*mum*
Papi	*dad*

Some related words/expressions

die Liebe	*love*
sich lieben	*to love one another/ to make love*
wir lieben uns	*we love one another/ we make love*
Ich liebe dich	*I love you*
sich verlieben	*to fall in love*
ich bin verliebt	*I am in love*
ich habe mich verliebt	*I fell in love*
die Liebenden	*lovers*
das Liebeswochenende	*romantic weekend*
das Liebeslied	*love song*
die Liebesgeschichte	*love story*
der Kummer	*the worry*
der Liebeskummer	*love sickness*
sie/er hat Liebeskummer	*s/he is love sick*
die Liebeserklärung	*declaration of love*
Sie machte ihm/ihr eine Liebeserklärung.	*She made him/her a declaration of love.*
er/sie ist verliebt	*he/she is in love*
das Herz	*the heart*
Herzchen	*sweetheart*

Herzlichen Glückwunsch   *congratulations*
Herzliche Grüße   *greetings/very best wishes*

2.2 Children

Core vocabulary

baby	das Baby (ies)
infant	der Säugling (e)
child	das Kind (er)
boy	der Junge (n)
girl	das Mädchen (-)
twin	der Zwilling
twins	die Zwillinge
teenager	der Teenager (-)
adolescent	der Jugendliche (n)
pregnancy	die Schwangerschaft (en)
birth	die Geburt (en)
newborn baby	das Neugeborene (n)
nanny	die Tagesmutter (¨)
childminder	die Kinderbetreuerin
babysitter	der Babysitter (-)
midwife	die Hebamme(n)
crèche	die Krippe (n)
playschool	der Hort (s)
baby's bottle	die Babyflasche (n)
teat	der Gummisauger (-)
dummy	der Schnuller (-)
bib	der Latz (¨e)
babymilk	die Babymilch
highchair	der Hochstuhl (¨e)
nappy	die Windel (n)
travel cot	das Reisebett (en)
cot	das Kinderbett (en)
pram	der Kinderwagen
pushchair	der Buggy (ies)
toy	das Spielzeug (e)
wind/colic	die Blähungen
an only child	ein Einzelkind (er)
an adopted child	ein adoptiertes Kind
an orphan	ein Waisenkind
children's playground	der Kinderspielplatz
swing	die Schaukel

slide	die Rutsche
climbing frame	das Klettergerüst

Useful verbs

to expect a baby	ein Baby erwarten
to breast feed	stillen
to burp	<u>auf</u>stoßen
to change a nappy	Windeln wechseln
to cry	weinen
to feed	füttern
to give a bottle	die Flasche geben
to rock	schaukeln
to teethe	zahnen
to look after	<u>auf</u>passen
to child mind	auf das Kind <u>auf</u>passen
to babysit	babysitten

Useful words and phrases

I am pregnant	ich bin schwanger
I'm on the pill	ich nehme die Pille
it's a boy/girl	es ist ein Junge/Mädchen
siblings	die Geschwister (pl)
family planning	die Familienplanung
a spoilt child	ein verwöhntes Kind
I need:	ich brauche:
a cream for a sore bottom	eine Wundcreme
sun cream/crème for babies	eine Sonnencreme/Babycreme
something for wind/teething	etwas gegen Blähungen/Zahnen

Compound words

das Kind	*child*	kindlich	*childlike*
kindisch	*childish*	die Kinder	*children*
der Garten		*garden*	
der Kindergarten		*kindergarten*	
die Kindergärtnerin		*child educator*	
der Kinderhort		*afterschool care*	
der Spielplatz		*playground*	
der Kinderspielplatz		*children's playground*	
das Kindermädchen		*au pair*	

2.3 Anniversaries, marriage and death

Core vocabulary

birthday	der Geburtstag
engagement	die Verlobung
marriage	die Hochzeit, die Heirat
death	der Tod
the wedding	die Hochzeit
church	die Kirche
register office	das Standesamt
engagement ring	der Verlobungsring
wedding invitation	die Hochzeitseinladung
wedding day	der Hochzeitstag
wedding dress	das Hochzeitskleid
wedding ceremony	die Trauung
wedding ring	der Ehering
wedding certificate	der Eheschein
wedding cake	der Hochzeitskuchen
bride	die Braut
bridegroom	der Bräutigam
bridesmaid	die Brautjungfer
honeymoon	die Hochzeitsreise
married life	die Ehe
separation	die Trennung
divorce	die Scheidung
heterosexual	heterosexuell
homosexual	homosexuell
lesbian	lesbisch
gay	schwul
death	der Tod
funeral	die Beerdigung
corpse	der Körper/die Leiche
coffin	der Sarg
cemetery	der Friedhof
burial	die Beerdigung
cremation	die Einäscherung
grave	das Grab
death certificate	der Totenschein
will	das Testament

Useful phrases

Congratulations!	Herzlichen Glückwunsch!
Happy birthday!	Herzlichen Glückwunsch zum Geburtstag!
Congratulations on your engagement/wedding!	Glückwünsche zu Ihrer/Eurer Verlobung/Hochzeit!
We would like to wish you every future happiness.	Wir wünschen Ihnen/euch für die Zukunft alles Liebe und Gute.
We would like to send you our best wishes.	Wir möchten unsere besten Wünsche übermitteln.
I would like to convey my condolences.	Herzliches Beileid.

Useful verbs

to get engaged	sich verloben
to get married	heiraten
to die	sterben
to bury	beerdigen
to be in mourning	trauern
to kill yourself	Selbstmord begehen
to be single	single sein
to propose	einen Heiratsantrag machen

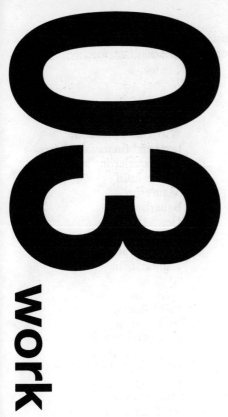

03

work

3.1 Job titles

i In English, you use the article, saying *I am a teacher*. In German, you say: **Ich bin Lehrerin** (drop the *a*) (literally, *I am teacher*).

Core vocabulary

I am a/n	Ich bin
accountant	Buchhalter/in
accountant	Wirtschaftsprüfer/in (external financial adviser)
actor/actress	Schauspieler/in
architect	Architekt/in
bricklayer	Maurer/in
builder	Bauarbeiter/in
businessman/woman	Geschäftsmann/ Geschäftsfrau
cleaner	die Putzfrau/mann
dentist	Zahnarzt/¨in
doctor	Arzt/¨in
driver	Fahrer/in
electrician	Elektriker/in
engineer	Ingenieur/in
farmer	Bauer/Bäuerin
fireman	Feuerwehrmann
housewife/househusband	Hausfrau/mann
hairdresser	Frisör/Frisörin
journalist	Journalist/in
lawyer	Rechtsanwalt/¨in
lecturer	Lehrer/in
mechanic	Mechaniker/in
musician	Musiker/in
nurse (f/m)	Krankenpfleger/in
plumber	Klempner/in
policeman	Polizist/in
postman	Postbeamte/in
receptionist	Emfangsdame/Emfangschef
scientist	Wissenschaftler/in
secretary	Sekretär/in
shop assistant	Verkäufer/in
shopkeeper	Ladenbesitzer/in
student	Student/in
waiter/waitress	Bedienung
waiter/waitress	Kellner/in
unemployed	arbeitslos

retired	in Rente
worker	Arbeiter/in
employer	Arbeitgeber/in
civil servant	Beamte/in
academic	Akademiker/in
business person	der/die Geschäftsmann/frau
self-employed person	Selbstständige/r
au pair	Au pair
chairman/woman	Vorsitzende/r
chief executive	Hauptgeschäftsführer/in
managing director	leitende/r Direktor/in
director	Direktor/in
company secretary	Prokurist/in
departmental head	Geschäftsführende/r Abteilungsleiter/in
manager/manageress	Geschäftsführer/in
manager of department	Abteilungsleiter/in
business consultant	Geschäftsberater/in
personal assistant	persönliche Assistentin
employer/employee	Angestellte/r
sales representative	Verkaufsleiter/in
computer operator	Computerbildschirmmit-arbeiter/in
computer programmer	Computerprogammierer/in
trainee	Auszubildende/r
person on work experience	Praktikant /in
full-time job	die Vollzeitarbeit
part-time work	die Halbtagsarbeit
job share	das Jobsharing
temporary and casual work	die befristete Arbeit
seasonal work	die Saisonarbeit

Useful words and phrases

I would like to work in ...	ich möchte in ... arbeiten.
I would like to work in a shoe shop.	Ich möchte in einem Schuhgeschäft arbeiten.
I would like to work as a ...	ich möchte als ... arbeiten.
I would like to work as a waitress.	Ich möchte als Kellnerin arbeiten.

I work in ...	*I work as a ...*
Ich arbeite ...	Ich arbeite als ...
agriculture in der Landwirtschaft	*farmer* Bauer/¨in
banking im Bankwesen	*clerk* Angestellte/r
building trade im Baugewerbe	*carpenter* Zimmermann
catering in der Gastronomie	*pub owner* Gastwirt/in
civil service im öffentlichen Dienst	*civil servant* Beamte/r
finance im Finanzwesen	*financial adviser* Finanzberater/in
the hotel industry in der Hotelindustrie	*hotelier* als Hotelier
insurance im Versicherungswesen	*sales agent* Versicherungsvertreter/in

I work in ...	Ich arbeite ...
services	in der Freizeitindustrie
manufacturing	in der Herstellungsindustrie
medicine	im medizinischen Bereich
the media	im Mediensektor, in den Medien
the public services	im öffentlichen Verkehrswesen
purchasing	im Einkaufsbereich
retail	im Einzelhandel
service industry	im Dienstleistungsbereich
show business	im Showgeschäft
textiles	in der Textilindustrie
tourism	im Tourismus
transport	im Verkehrswesen
wholesale	im Großhandel

Useful verbs

to work/gain a living	arbeiten/jobben/meinen Lebensunterhalt erwerben
to be out of work	ohne festen Arbeitsplatz sein
to buy/sell	kaufen/verkaufen
to import/export	importieren/exportieren
to manage	managen/leiten
to manufacture	herstellen
to communicate	kommunizieren
to phone	telefonieren/<u>an</u>rufen
to negotiate	verhandeln
to develop	entwickeln

to build	bauen
to sew	nähen
to clean	putzen
to research	forschen

Related words to do with employment

das Beschäftigungs-verhältnis (se)	*employment*
die Arbeitslosigkeit	*unemployment*
der Arbeitnehmer (-)	*employee*
der Angestellte (n)	*salaried employee*
<u>an</u>stellen	*to employ*
angestellt	*employed*
arbeitslos	*unemployed*
arbeitswillig	*willing to work*
arbeitsunwillig	*unwilling to work*
der Arbeiter (-)	*worker/labourer*
der Arbeitsplatz (¨e)	*place of work*
freie Arbeitsplätze	*vacancies*
die Arbeitsatmosphäre	*working atmosphere*
die Arbeitsbedingungen	*working conditions*
die Arbeitskleidung	*working clothes*
die Arbeitsteilung	*division of labour*
die Arbeitsüberlastung	*overworking*
die Aushilfe (n)	*temporary staff*
nach Arbeitsschluss	*after working hours*
die Bundesanstalt für Arbeit	*the German Federal Labour Office*
die/der Beschäftigte (n)	*employee*
die/das Beschäftigungs-verhältnis (se)	*working conditions*
beschäftigt sein bei	*to be employed with*
der Streik (s)	*strike*
streiken	*to strike*
die Schwarzarbeit(-)	*illegal work*

3.2 Where do you work?

Core vocabulary

I work in a ...	Ich arbeite ...
bank	in einer Bank
factory	in einer Fabrik
farm	auf einem Bauernhof

garage	in einer Werkstatt
hospital	in einem Krankenhaus
hotel	in einem Hotel
mine	in einer Mine
office	in einem Büro
post office	auf einer Post
railway	bei der Bahn
restaurant	in einem Restaurant
school	in einer Schule
service station	an einer Tankstelle
shopping centre	in einem Einkaufszentrum
studio	in einem Studio
town hall	in einem Rathaus
workshop	in einer Werkstatt

The company

headquarters	die Hauptgeschäftsstelle
subsidiary	die Tochtergesellschaft
firm	die Firma/Firmen
factory	die Fabrik (en)
branch	die Zweigstelle (n)
I work in an office	Ich arbeite in einem Büro
on a building site	auf einer Baustelle
in a workshop	in einer Werkstatt
in a factory	in einer Fabrik
outside	draußen
the premises	die Räumlichkeiten
boardroom	das Konferenzzimmer
canteen	die Kantine
meeting room	das Besprechungszimmer
reception	die Rezeption
entrance	der Eingang
exit	der Ausgang
I work in the ... department.	Ich arbeite in ... Abteilung.
accounts	der Buchhaltungsabteilung
advertising	der Werbeabteilung
administration	der Verwaltung
catering	der Gastronomie
distribution	der Verteilung
export/import	der Export-Importabteilung
information technology	Informatikabteilung
insurance	Versicherungsabteilung
legal	Rechtsabteilung

manufacturing	Herstellungsabteilung
marketing	Marketingabteilung
personnel/human resources	Personalabteilung
property	Grundstücksabteilung
purchasing	Einkaufsabteilung
sales	Verkaufsabteilung
technical	technischen Abteilung

Useful phrases

I would like to speak to Mr/Mrs Braun.	Ich möchte gerne Frau/Herrn Braun sprechen.
I have an appointment with Mr/Mrs Braun.	Ich habe einen Termin mit Herrn/Frau Braun.
Mr/Mrs Braun is still in a meeting.	Herr/Frau Braun ist noch in einer Besprechung.
Do you wish to wait?	Möchten Sie warten?
Yes, please.	Ja gerne.
Please sit down.	Bitte nehmen Sie Platz.
Can I get you a coffee?	Möchten Sie eine Tasse Kaffee?

There is often one part of the word that can give you a clue to its meaning or help you to remember it. So don't worry about long words in German: all you have to do is break them up:

Arbeitsunfähigkeitsbescheinigung

die Arbeit (n)/der Job	*the work/job*
die Unfähigkeit	*inability*
die Bescheinigung (en)	*certificate*
die Arbeitsunfähigkeits- bescheinigung	*certificate to prove inability to work*

More compound words

das Amt ("er)	*the office*
das Arbeitsamt	*the job centre*
der/die Angestellte (n)	*employee*
der/die Arbeitsamtsangestelle	*employee working for the job centre*
vermitteln	*to arrange*
die Arbeitsvermittlung	*arranging employment*
die Erlaubnis	*permission*

die Arbeitserlaubnis *work permit*
geben *to give:* der Arbeitsgeber *employer*
nehmen *to take:* der Arbeitnehmer *employee*
die Tagung *conference:* die Arbeitgebertagung
conference for employers

an extremely hard-working person ein Arbeitstier Tier = *animal*
Er/sie ist ein richtiges Arbeitstier. *He/she is a working animal.*
Ihn/sie hat die Arbeitswut *He/she turned into an*
gepackt. *workoholic.*

Useful verbs

to buy	kaufen	gekauft
to manage	managen/leiten	gemanegt/geleitet
to manufacture	herstellen	hergestellt
to research	forschen	geforscht
to sell	verkaufen	verkauft
to study	studieren	studiert
to travel	reisen	gereist
to work	arbeiten	gearbeitet

3.3 Conditions of employment

Core vocabulary

working conditions	die Arbeitsbedingungen
the working day	der Arbeitstag (e)
the working week	die Arbeitswoche
holidays	die Ferien (-)
annual holiday	der jährliche Urlaub
national holidays	die Feiertage
pay	die Bezahlung
salary	das Gehalt ("er)
income	das Einkommen (-)
income tax	die Einkommenssteuer
VAT	die Mehrwehrtssteuer MwSt.
wages	der Lohn ("e)
applicant	der/die Bewerber/in (nen)
application	die Bewerbung (en)
application form	das Bewerbungsformular (e)
CV	der Lebenslauf ("e)

contract	der Vertrag (¨e)
job interview	das Interview(s)
full-time job	die Vollzeitstelle (n)
part-time job	die Teilzeitstelle (n)
job share	Jobshare/die halbe Stelle
part time	die Teilzeitstelle (n)
office hours	die Bürostunden
overtime	die Überstunden
flexitime	die flexiblen Arbeitsstunden
coffee break	die Kaffeepause (n)
lunchtime	die Mittagspause (n)
closing time for shops	der Ladenschluss
opening hours for shops	die Ladenöffnungszeiten

ℹ Typical signs you find on the door of a shop or an office:

Heute geschlossen	closed today
Montags geschlossen	Mondays closed
Mittagspause	closed for lunch
Bald zurück	back soon
Bürostunden sind ... Uhr bis ... Uhr	

holiday entitlement	der Urlaubsanspruch
sick leave	die Krankenbeurlaubung (en)
sick note	die Krankenbescheinigung/(en) (die Arbeitsunfähigkeitsbescheinigung (en))
redundancy payment	die Abfindung (en)

ℹ There is one word in German to cover both dismissal and redundancy: **Die Entlassung: Der Personalchef ist entlassen worden** can mean either that he was dismissed or that he was made redundant.

union	die Gewerkschaft (en)
union meeting	die Gewerkschaftsversammlung (en)
strike	der Streik (s)
demand	die Forderung (en)
bankruptcy	der Bankrott
standard of living	der Lebenstandard
unemployment rate	die Arbeitslosenrate (n)
legal minimum wage	der Mindestlohn (¨e)

Useful words and phrases

It is stressful/stimulating/ motivating	Es ist sehr stressig/ stimulierend/motivierend
He/she is very	er/sie ist sehr
efficient	fähig
organized/disorganized	organisiert/unorganisiert
hard working/lazy	fleißig/faul

Useful verbs

to be behind with one's work	mit der Arbeit hinterher hinken
to have a deadline	einen Abgabetermin haben
to be overworked	überarbeitet sein
to be stressed	gestresst sein
to be a lot of work	viel Arbeit machen
to do a good job	gründliche Arbeit leisten

3.4 Writing a letter

Addressing somebody in a formal letter

Ways to start a letter

Sehr geehrte Damen und Herren,	(best way of writing to a company when you don't know a specific name)
Sehr geehrte Herren,	(only when you know for sure there are only men)
Sehr geehrte Damen,	(only when you know for sure there are only women)
Sehr geehrte Frau Meier, Sehr geehrter Herr Braun,	(if you know the person's name)
Sehr geehrte Frau Schmidt, sehr geehrter Herr Meier,	(writing to two different people)
Vielen Dank für …	*Many thanks for …*
Wir haben … erhalten	*We received …*
Hiermit möchte ich mich recht herzlich bei Ihnen für … bedanken.	*I would like to thank you for …*
Wir möchten uns erkundigen, ob …	*We are writing to ask whether …*

In Bezug auf Ihr Schreiben vom ...,	*Regarding your letter of ...*
Bezugnehmend zu unserem Telefonat ...	*Regarding our telephone call ...*
Ich beziehe mich auf ...	*In reply to ...*
Wir bedauern sehr, dass ...	*We regret that ...*
Wir bestätigen den Erhalt ... (followed by genitive)	*We acknowledge the receipt of ...*

Ways to end a formal letter

Mit freundlichen Grüßen
Mit besten Grüßen
Mit besten Empfehlungen
Hochachtungsvoll (very formal)

Ich stehe Ihnen gerne für weitere Informationen zur Verfügung.	*Please don't hesitate to contact me for further information.*
Wir freuen uns auf Ihre baldige Antwort.	*We are looking forward to your early reply.*
Ich würde mich sehr freuen, bald wieder von Ihnen zu hören.	*I look forward to hearing from you soon.*
Ich hoffe, bald wieder von Ihnen zu hören.	*Hoping to hear from you soon.*
... und verbleibe mit freundlichen Grüßen	*and remain yours ...*

Addressing someone in an informal letter

Ways to start/close an informal letter

Liebe Susanne,	*Dear Susanne*
Lieber Stefan,	*Dear Stefan*
Alles Liebe von ...	*Love from ...*
Alles Liebe und Gute	*All my love and best wishes*
Viele Grüße	*Best wishes*
Grüße, Deine/Dein ...	*Best wishes, your ...*
Ich freue mich, bald wieder von Dir zu hören.	*I am looking forward to hearing from you soon.*
Dein Klaus	*Your Klaus*
Deine Claudia	*Your Claudia*

Other informal letter endings:

Mach's gut.	*Take care.*
Bis bald.	*See you soon.*
Ruf mal an.	*Phone me.*
Schreib mal wieder.	*Write to me again.*

3.5 Using the telephone

Core vocabulary

telephone	das Telefon (e)
receiver	der Hörer (-)
extension	der Apparat (e)
mobile	das Handy (s)
telephone number	die Telefonnummer (n)
directory	das Telefonbuch (¨er)
local call	das Ortsgespräch (e)
long distance call	das Ferngespräch (e)
international call	der internationale Anruf (e)
answering machine	der Anrufbeantworter (-)

Useful words and phrases

Could I speak to Mr/Mrs ...?	Könnte ich bitte Frau/Herrn ... sprechen?
Can I have extension ... please?	Bitte verbinden Sie mich mit Apparat ...?
Who can help me regarding ...?	Wer kann mir mit ... helfen?
Who is calling?	Wer ist dort bitte?
Can you tell me what it is about?	Können Sie mir sagen, worum es sich handelt?
To whom would you like to speak?	Mit wem möchten Sie sprechen?
Speaking!	Am Apparat!
Can you wait a moment?	Können Sie einen Moment warten?
I am putting you through.	Ich stelle Sie jetzt durch.
The line is engaged.	Der Apparat ist besetzt.
busy	besetzt
free	frei
Do you want to hold?	Möchten Sie warten?
Would you like to leave a message?	Möchten Sie eine Nachricht hinterlassen?
Can I take your name and number?	Könnte ich bitte Ihren Namen und Ihre Telefonnummer haben?
My battery is running low.	Meine Batterie ist leer.
Can you ring back?	Könnten Sie zurückrufen?
Can you text me?	Könnten Sie es mir bitte texten?

Answerphone messages

Hier ist der telefonische Anrufbeantworter Schmidt. Wir sind zur Zeit leider nicht erreichbar, aber wenn Sie eine Nachricht hinterlassen wollen, sprechen Sie bitte nach dem Ton.
This is the telephone answering machine of Mr/Mrs Schmidt. Unfortunately you cannot reach us at present but if you wish to leave a message, please speak after the tone.

Es tut mir Leid, wir sind zur Zeit nicht erreichbar, aber Sie können eine Nachricht hinterlassen.
I am sorry, but we are not available at present, but you may leave a message.

Unsere Öffnungszeiten sind montags bis freitags von 8 Uhr bis 16 Uhr. Sie können uns gerne eine Nachricht hinterlassen, wir rufen Sie umgehend zurück.
Our opening hours are Mondays to Fridays from 8 am to 4 pm. You can leave a message and we will phone you back immediately.

Useful verbs

to phone	<u>an</u>rufen
to call	telefonieren
to call back	<u>zurück</u>rufen
to dial	wählen
to put someone through	<u>durch</u>stellen/verbinden
to look up a number	eine Nummer <u>nach</u>schauen
to leave a message	eine Nachricht <u>hinter</u>lassen

3.6 Using the computer

Core vocabulary

computer	der Computer (-)
keyboard	die Tastatur (en)
mouse	die Maus
microphone	das Mikrofon (e)
speakers	die Lautsprecher (-)
hard drive	die Festplatte (n)
worldwide web	das Web
net	das Netz
password	das Passwort (¨er)
program	das Programm (e)
modem	das Modem (-)
battery	die Batterie (n)
search engine	die Suchmaschine (n)

screen	der Bildschirm (e)
laptop	der Laptop (s)
printer	der Drucker (-)
scanner	der Scanner (-)
server	der Bediener (-)
mail box	die Mailbox (en)
junk mail	die Junkmail
Word	Word
email	die E-Mail (s)

Useful words and phrases

Have you got a/an …?	Haben Sie …?
internet connection	einen Internetanschluss
Word 2000	Word 2000
a CD-ROM	eine CD-ROM
Where can I plug in my laptop?	Wo kann ich meinen Laptop einstecken?
My computer isn't working.	Mein Computer geht nicht.
Is there anyone who can help me?	Kann mir irgendjemand helfen?
I log on.	Ich logge mich <u>ein</u>.

Useful verbs

to switch on	<u>an</u>stellen
to type in	tippen
to log on	<u>ein</u>loggen
to log off	<u>ab</u>schalten
to save	speichern
to go online	<u>ein</u>schalten
to send an email	eine E-Mail schicken
to receive mail	eine E-Mail erhalten
to download a file	die Datei <u>herunterladen</u>
to recharge the battery	die Batterie <u>auf</u>laden
to fill in	<u>ein</u>tragen
to text a message	eine Nachricht texten

i Words you'll come across on your computer screen

das Word	*Word*	Format	*Format*
die Datei	*File*	Extras	*Tools*
bearbeiten	*Edit*	Tabelle	*Table*
Ansicht	*View*	Fenster	*Windows*
<u>ein</u>fügen	*Insert*	Extras	*Help*

04

education

4.1 Primary and secondary education

i The school-leaving certificate is called:

from Hauptschule: **Hauptschulabschluss**
from Realschule: **Realschulabschluss**
from Gesamtschule: **Realschulabschluss** or **Abitur**
from Gymnasium: **Abitur**.

Pupils stay for 5 or 6 years in **Hauptschule** and usually enter an apprenticeship (**Lehre**) after that. They can also study for vocational qualifications at a **Berufsschule**. From **Realschule** pupils can enter an apprenticeship or go into further education (**Fachschulen**). **Gymnasium** concludes with the **Abitur** that awards the **Zeugnis der allgemeinen Hochschulreife** (university entrance qualifications).

Core vocabulary

headmaster	Schuldirektor/in
deputy head	stellvertretende/r Direktor/in
secondary teacher	Hauptschullehrer/in
secondary school teacher	Realschullehrer/in
grammar school teacher	Gymnasialleher/in
primary teacher	Grundschullehrer/in
pupil	Schüler/in
the school secretary	Schulsekretär/in
the school caretaker	der Hausmeister (-)
lesson	der Unterricht
break	die Pause (n)
bell	die Schulglocke (n)
end of lessons	das Ende der Stunde
term	das Schuljahr (e)
halfterm	das Halbjahr (e)
holidays	die Ferien
timetable	der Stundenplan (¨e)
school subjects	die Schulfächer

art	Kunst	*IT*	Informatik
biology	Biologie	*Latin*	Latein
chemistry	Chemie	*maths*	Mathematik
English	Englisch	*music*	Musik
French	Französisch	*PE*	Sport
history	Geschichte	*physics*	Physik
geography	Erdkunde	*Spanish*	Spanisch
German	Deutsch	*Technology*	Technologie

building	das Schulgebäude (-)
classroom	das Klassenzimmer (-)
corridor	der Flur (e)
science lab	das Labor (e)
gym	die Turnhalle (n)
music room	der Musikraum (¨e)
library	die Bücherei (en)
computer room	der Computerraum (¨e)
changing room	der Umkleideraum (¨e)
toilets	die Toiletten
girls'/boys' toilets	die Toiletten Mädchen/Jungen
desk	der Schultisch (e)
blackboard	die Tafel (n)
projector	der Projektor (en)
computer	der Computer (-)
overhead projector	der Overhead-Projektor (en)
book	das Buch (¨er)
chalk	die Kreide (-)
exercise book	das Schulheft (e)
pencil case	die Federmappe (n)
pen	der Kuli (s)
pencil	der Bleistift (e)
eraser	das Radiergummi (s)
calculator	der Taschenrechner (-)
ruler	das Lineal (e)
report	das Zeugnis (e)
school bag	die Schultasche (n)
sports kit	das Sportzeug (-)

Useful words and phrases

to do homework	Hausaufgaben machen
to get a good mark	gute Noten bekommen
to sit an exam	eine Prüfung machen
to pass a test	bestehen
to fail a test	<u>durch</u>fallen
to resit	<u>wieder</u>holen
a pupil who has to repeat one whole class	Wiederholer
having to repeat a whole year	·sitzenbleiben

| an intelligent pupil who can miss out one whole school year and goes one class up | Überspringer |
| to miss out one school year | ein Jahr springen |

Useful verbs

to read	lesen
to speak	sprechen
to listen	hören
to talk	sprechen
to discuss	diskutieren
to write	schreiben
to copy	kopieren
to take notes	<u>mit</u>schreiben
to be quiet	ruhig sein

i The grading scale runs from **eins** (the best mark) to **sechs** (**fünf** in Austria). Students who have a five or six in several subjects have to repeat a whole year (**sitzenbleiben**).

4.2 Further and higher education

i There are various types of colleges, universities and courses:

die Volkshochschule (n)	various leisure classes
die Berufsschule (n)	vocational college
die Fachschule (n)	technical college
die Fachhochschule (n)	polytechnic
die Universität (en)	
die Hochschule (n)	university
der Universitätsabschluss (¨e)	degree
der Studiengang (¨e)	degree course
Wirtschaftswissenschaft (en)	economics
Rechtswissenschaft (en)	law
Naturwissenschaften	science
Sozialwissenschaften	social science
Sprachwissenschaften	linguistics
Betriebswirtschaftslehre	business management
Zahnmedizin	dentistry
Philosophie	philosophy
Psychologie	psychology

Core vocabulary

university	die Universität (en)
faculty	die Fakultät (en)
lecture	die Vorlesung (en)
seminar	das Seminar (e)
tutorial	das Kolloqium
subject	das Studienfach (¨er)
professor	Professor/in (en) (nen)
lecturer	die Lehrkraft (¨e)
student	Student/in (en) (nen)
research assistant	Forschungsassistent/in
graduate	Hochschulabsolvent/in (en) (nen)
undergraduate	Student/Studentin (en) (nen)
apprenticeship	die Lehre (n)
trainee	der/die Auszubildende (n)
examination	das Examen (-)/die Prüfung (en)
curriculum	der Lehrplan (¨e)
teacher training	der Lehramtsstudiengang (¨e)
mark	die Note (n)
grade	die Note (n)
research	die Forschung (en)
paper	das Referat (e)
report	der Bericht (e)
dissertation	die Dissertation (en)/die Doktorarbeit (en)
thesis for diploma	die Diplomarbeit (en)
to present a paper	ein Referat halten über
to do a sandwich course	theoretischer und praktischer Ausbildungsgang
to study part-time	Teilzeitstudium
to attend evening class	Abendunterricht besuchen
to do work experience	Arbeitspraktikum machen
to miss a deadline	einen Termin verpassen

Useful words and phrases

das Studium/Studien	*studies*
der Studienanfänger (-)	*first-year student*
der Studienaufenthalt (e)	*study visit*

der Studienabschluss (¨e)	*completion*
das Studienfach (¨er)	*subject at university*
der Studiengang (¨e)	*university, college degree course*
die Studienordnung (en)	*course regulation*
der Studienplatz(¨e)	*university/college place*
ein Studium aufnehmen/beginnen	*to begin one's studies*
während seines Studiums …	*while he was/is a student*
sich für einen Studiengang bewerben	*to apply for a degree course*
die Immatrikulation (en)	*registration, matriculation*
sich immatrikulieren	*to register*
das Immatrikulationsbüro (s)	*registration office*
die Immatrikulations- bescheinigung (en)	*registration certificate*
die Doktorwürde verliehen bekommen	*to get one's doctorate*
Sie sitzt immer noch <u>an</u> ihrer Doktorarbeit.	*She is still doing her doctorate*
Er hat einen Doktortitel in Sozialwissenschaften.	*He has a doctorate in social science.*
der/die Prüfer/in (-) (nen)	*examiner*
eine Prüfung bestehen	*to pass an exam*
eine Prüfung wiederholen	*to repeat an exam*
durch eine Prüfung durchfallen	*to fail an exam*
eine Prüfung vorbereiten	*to prepare for an exam*

Useful verbs

to correct	korrigieren
to discuss	diskutieren
to explain	erklären
to learn	lernen
to qualify	qualifizieren
to register/enrol	<u>ein</u>schreiben
to study	studieren
to teach	unterrichten
to translate	übersetzen
to understand	verstehen
to do research	Forschung betreiben

05 at home

5.1 The house

ℹ Zu vermieten

U-Näh, 2-Zi.-Whg, Kü.- u Badbenutz. vollmöbl. 600 Eur – inkl. Nebenk. 96m, Kaut. 5.OG, Aufzg, gr. SW-Blk. Verm. Tel: 339281048

U-Näh = Universitäts-Nähe	*near the university*
Zi = Zimmer	*room(s)*
Whg = Wohnung	*flat*
Kü. = Küche	*kitchen*
benutz = Benutzung	*shared*
vollmöbl. = vollmöbliert	*fully furnished*
Nebenk. = die Nebenkosten	*rates for gas, electricity*
Kaut. = Kaution	*deposit*
OG = Obergeschoss	*floor*
Aufzg = Aufzug	*lift*
gr. = großer	*large*
SW = Südwest	*southwest*
Blk = Balkon	*balcony*
Verm. = Vermieter	*landlord*

ℹ Zu verkaufen:

Exklus. Einfamilienhaus im Landhausstil, ruh. Lage, am Stadtr. 5-Zi, 2 Bäder, Kamine, Wintergarten, Terr., Whirlpool, Sauna, 699000 Euro + Prov. ca.345qm Wohnfl., Fußbodenheiz., Doppelfenst. traumh. gepfl. Garten absolute Ruhiglg. Immoblienmakler Sauer
Tel. 758493827

exklus. = exklusiv	*exclusive*
ruh. = ruhig	*quiet*
Stadtr. = der Stadtrand	*outskirts*
Terr. = die Terrasse	*terrace*
Prov. = die Provision	*commission*
Fußbodenheiz. = Fußboden-heizung	*underfloor heating*
Doppelfenst. = Doppelfenster	*doubleglazing*
traumh. = traumhafter	*beautiful*
gepfl. = gepflegt	*well looked after*
Ruhiglg. = Ruhiglage	*quiet position*

Core vocabulary

house	das Haus ("er)
home	das Zuhause
apartment	das Apartment (s)

flat	die Wohnung (en)
studio flat	die Apartmentwohnung
block of flats	das Wohnhaus (¨er)
the building	das Gebäude (-)
floor/storey	die Etage (n)/das Geschoss (e)
ground floor	das Erdgeschoss
first floor	die erste Etage/der erste Stock
second floor	die zweite Etage/der zweite Stock
basement	das Untergeschoss
attic	der Boden (¨-)
stairs	die Treppen
lift	der Lift (e), der Aufzug (¨e), der Fahrstuhl (¨)
garage	die Garage (n)
cellar	der Keller (-)
estate agent	der Makler/in
advertisement	die Anzeige (n)
for sale	zu verkaufen
for rent	zu vermieten
cottage	das Landhaus (¨er)
farm	das Bauernhaus (¨er)/der Bauernhof (¨e)
chalet	das Chalet (s)
villa	die Villa (Villen)
council flat	die Sozialwohnung (en)
detached house	das Einfamilienhaus
semi-detached house	das Zweifamilienhaus
terraced house	das Reihenhaus
bungalow	der Bungalow(s)
central heating	die Zentralheizung (en)
doubleglazing	das Doppelfenster
gas	das Gas
electricity	die Elektrizität
oil	das Öl
water	das Wasser
telephone	das Telefon (e)
mains sewerage	die Hauptabwasseranlage (n)
septic tank	der Klärbehälter (-)
soundproofing	schallgedämpft
insulation	die Isolierung (en)
shutters	die Fensterläden
burglar alarm	der Einbrecheralarm
fire alarm	der Feueralarm

outside	draußen
balcony	der Balkon (e)
roof	das Dach (¨er)
slates	die Ziegel
terrace	die Terrasse (n)
conservatory	der Wintergarten (¨)
garden	der Garten (¨)
gate	das Tor (e)
path	der Weg (e)
lawn	der Rasen (-)
flower bed	das Blumenbeet (e)
vegetable garden	der Gemüsegarten (¨)
greenhouse	das Gewächshaus (¨er)
the situation	die Lage (n)
view	die Aussicht (en)
stone	der Steine (-)
brick	der Ziegelstein (e)
timber	das Holz (¨er)
concrete	der Zement

Useful words and phrases

it overlooks the lake	mit Blick über den See
a central position	eine zentrale Lage
close to all services	zentrale Lage für Einkauf- und Verkehrsmittel
in the town centre	im Stadtzentrum
in the suburbs	im Außenbezirk
in the country	auf dem Land
to rent	mieten
the rent	die Miete
tenant	der/die Mieter/in
a contract	ein Vertrag
a lease	ein Mietvertrag
to sign a lease	einen Mietvertrag abschließen
to cancel a lease	einen Mietvertrag auflösen
to terminate lease	einen Mietvertrag kündigen
rented flat	die Mietwohnung (en)
block of flats	das Mietshaus (en)
increase	die Erhöhung
rent increase	die Mieterhöhung
to demand a rent increase	eine Mieterhöhung verlangen

tenancy	das Mietverhältnis (se)
arrears	der Rückstand ("e)
rent arrears	die Mietrückstände
the law	das Recht
rent law	das Mietrecht
to rent a house	ein Haus mieten
to get back the deposit	die Mietkaution zurückerhalten
the landlord	der/die Vermieter/in
letting	die Vermietung
to let	vermieten
rentable	vermietbar
Do you rent rooms?	Vermieten Sie Zimmer?

Useful verbs

to buy	kaufen
to sell	verkaufen
to rent	mieten
to view (a house)	besichtigen
to make an appointment	einen Termin vereinbaren

5.2 Rooms

Core vocabulary

room	das Zimmer (-)
entrance	der Eingang ("e)
kitchen	die Küche (n)
dining room	das Esszimmer
sitting room	das Wohnzimmer
bedroom	das Schlafzimmer
play room	das Kinderzimmer
bathroom	das Badezimmer
guest toilet	die Gästetoilette (n)
study/office	das Studienzimmer/das Büro (s)
shower	die Dusche (n)
hall	die Eingangshalle (n)
stairs	die Treppe (n)
utility room	die Vorratskammer (n)
junk room	die Abstellkammer (n)
window	das Fenster (-)

radiator	der Heizkörper (-)
floor	der Fußboden (¨)
foot	der Fuß
floor or attic	der Boden
ceiling	die Decke (n)
door	die Tür (en)
wall	die Wand (¨e)
window sill	das Fensterbrett (er)
heating	die Heizung
underfloor heating	die Fußbodenheizung
central heating	die Zentralheizung
gas	das Gas
electricity	die Elektrizität
oil	das Öl
doubleglazing	die Doppelfenster
solar-powered heating	die Solarenergieheizung
lock	das Schloss (¨er)
key	der Schlüssel (-)
plug	der Stecker (-)
socket	die Steckdose (n)
switch	der Schalter (-)
handle	der Griff (e)
fuse box	der Sicherungskasten (¨)
fuse	die Sicherung (en)
fuse wire	das Sicherungskabel (-)
torch	die Taschenlampe (n)
curtains	die Gardinen
blinds	die Rollos
shutters	die Rolläden
carpet	der Teppichboden (¨)
rug	der Läufer (-)
tiles	die Fliesen
flooring	der Bodenbelag (¨e)
wallpaper	die Tapete (n)
paint	die Farbe (n)
paintbrush	der Pinsel (-)
ladder	die Leiter (n)

Useful words and phrases

upstairs	oben
downstairs	unten
on the first floor	im ersten Stock

in the basement	im Erdgeschoss
in the attic	auf dem Boden
Where is the ...?	Wo ist ...?
How does it work?	Wie geht das?
to turn on/off	<u>auf</u>drehen/<u>ab</u>drehen
to switch on/off	<u>an</u>schalten/<u>ab</u>schalten
The floor has to be cleaned.	Der Fußboden muss gereinigt werden.

5.3 Furniture

Core vocabulary

furniture	die Möbel
sitting room	das Wohnzimmer (-)
armchair	der Sessel (-)
settee	das Sofa (s)
couch	die Couch (s)
three-piece suite	die Sitzgarnitur (en)
coffee table	der Wohnzimmertisch (e)
bookcase	das Bücherregal (e)
lamp	die Lampe (n)
picture	das Bild (er)
bedroom	das Schlafzimmer (-)
bed	das Bett (en)
chair	der Stuhl (¨e)
wardrobe	der Schrank (¨e)
chest of drawers	die Kommode (n)
mirror	der Spiegel (-)
built-in cupboard	der Einbauschrank (¨e)
shelves	das Regal (e)
bathroom	das Badezimmer (-)
bath	das Bad (¨er)
mirror	der Spiegel (-)
razor	der Rasierapparat (e)
shower	die Dusche (n)
wash basin	das Waschbecken (-)
toilet	die Toilette (n)
toothbrush	die Zahnbürste (n)
toothpaste	die Zahnpasta (s)

television	der Fernseher (-)
video recorder	der Videoapparat (e)
DVD player	der DVD-Spieler (-)
remote control	die Fernbedienung (en)
bedding	das Bettzeug (pl)
pillow/pillow case	das Kissen (-)
quilt	die Steppdecke (n), das Federbett (en)
quilt cover	die Bettdecke (n)
sheet	das Laken (-)
fitted sheet	das Spannbetttuch (¨er)
bath	das Badezimmer (-)
wash basin	das Waschbecken (-)
taps	der Wasserhahn (¨e)
plug	der Stecker (-)
shampoo	das Shampoo (s)
conditioner	die Pflegespülung (en)
hairdryer	der Fön (e)
soap	die Seife (n)
towel	das Handtuch (¨er)
deodorant	das Deodorant (s)
vacuum cleaner	der Staubsauger (-)
duster	das Staubtuch (¨er)
brush	die Bürste (n)
cleaning materials	das Reinigunsmaterial (ien)
scrubbing brush	die Scheuerbürste (n)
floor mop	der Fußbodenwischer (-)
detergent	der Reiniger (-)

Useful words and phrases

Where is the …?	Wo ist …?
It's on the table	Es ist auf dem Tisch
under the bed	unter dem Bett
in the armchair	auf dem Sessel
in the cupboard/drawer	in dem Schrank/in der Kommode
Can I have a clean …?	Kann ich ein sauberes … haben?
How does the (television) work?	Wie funktioniert der Fernseher?

Er muss den Müll in der Küche in getrennte Abfalleimer tun.	*He has to separate the rubbish in the kitchen into separate rubbish bins.*
Sie hat die Treppe nicht richtig gereinigt.	*She did not clean the stairs properly.*
Die Möbel sollten wirklich auf Hochglanz gebracht werden.	*The furniture should really be highly polished.*
Die Tischdecken hat sie nicht richtig gebügelt.	*She did not iron the tablecloths properly.*
Die Wohnung befindet sich in einem einwandfreien Zustand.	*The flat is in immaculate condition.*

Useful verbs

to do housework	die Hausarbeit machen
to wash	waschen
to clean	sauber machen
to do the vacuuming	<u>staub</u>saugen
to make the beds	die Betten machen

5.4 In the kitchen

Core vocabulary

in the kitchen	in der Küche
table	der Tisch (e)
chair	der Stuhl (¨e)
stool	der Hocker (-)
drawer	die Schublade (n)
cupboard	der Schrank (¨e)
shelf	das Regal (e)
sink	das Waschbecken (-)
fridge	der Kühlschrank (¨e)
dishwasher	der Geschirrspüler (-)
washing machine	die Waschmaschine (n)
dryer	der Trockner (-)
mixer	die Rührmaschine (n)
liquidizer	das Mixgerät (e)
plate	der Teller (-)
dinner plate	der Essteller (-)
bowl	die Schüssel (n)
dishes	das Geschirr

cup	die Tasse (n)
saucer	die Untertasse (n)
mug	der Becher (-)
jug	die Kanne (n)
teapot	die Teekanne (n)
sugar bowl	die Zuckerdose (n)
knife	das Messer (-)
fork	die Gabel (n)
spoon	der Löffel (-)
salt	das Salz
pepper	der Pfeffer
mustard	der Senf
teaspoon	der Teelöffel (-)
soup spoon	der Suppenlöffel (-)
dessert spoon	der Esslöffel (-)
serving spoon	der Vorlegelöffel (-)
carving knife	das Tranchiermesser (-)
bread knife	das Brotmesser (-)
sharp knife	ein scharfes Messer (-)
glass	das Glas (¨er)
wineglass	das Weinglas (¨er)
champagne flute	das Champagnerglas (¨er)
water glass	das Wasserglas (¨er)
tumbler	der Becher (-)

I like/dislike cooking.	Ich koche gerne/nicht gerne.
I'll do the washing up.	Ich mache den Abwasch.
I'll take the rubbish out.	Ich bringe den Abfall raus.

Useful verbs

Cooking terms *Kochanleitungen*

to mix	mischen/vermischen
to beat	schlagen
to roast	rösten
to toast	toasten
to bake	backen
to steam	dämpfen
to grill	grillen
to barbecue	grillen
to peel	pellen
to cut	schneiden
to slice	in Scheiben schneiden
to chop	hacken

Dealing with waste

rubbish	der Müll
leftovers	die Essensreste
packaging	die Verpackungen
plastic bags	die Plastiktüten
kitchen bin/waste bin	der Abfalleimer
bin liner	die Abfalltüten
dustbin	der Staubbeutel
recycling	das Recycling
bottle bank	der Glaskontainer
paper bank	der Papierkontainer
compost	der Küchenabfall
clothes bank	die Kleidertonne

5.5 Outside

Core vocabulary

garage	die Garage (n)
shed	der Schuppen (-)
footpath	der Gartenweg (e)
gate	das Gartentor (e)
in the garden	in dem Garten
flower bed	das Blumenbeet (e)
lawn	der Rasen (-)
flower	die Blume (n)
plant	die Pflanze (n)
bush	der Busch (¨e)
shrub	der Strauch (¨er)
tree	der Baum (¨e)
grass	das Gras (¨er)
weeds	das Unkraut (¨er)
herb	das Gewürz (e)
bulb	die Blumenzwiebel (n)

Types of tree

beech	die Buche (n)
birch	die Birke (n)
chestnut	der Kastanienbaum (¨e)
oak	die Eiche (n)
holly	die Stechpalme (n)
lime tree	der Lindenbaum (¨e)

oak	die Eiche (n)
willow	die Weide (n)
pine	die Tanne (n)

Types of flower

carnation	die Nelke (n)
daffodil	die Osterglocke (n)
lily	die Lilie (n)
narcissus	die Narzisse (n)
pansy	das Stiefmütterchen (-)
rose	die Rose (n)
sunflower	die Sonnenblume (n)
tulip	die Tulpe (n)

Tools, etc.

garden tools	das Gartengerät (e)
rake	die Harke (n)
spade	der Spaten (-)
lawnmower	der Rasenmäher (-)
strimmer	der Rasentrimmer (-)
wheelbarrow	die Schubkarre (n)
garden tractor	der Gartentraktor (en)
hose	der Gartenschlauch (¨e)
sprinkler	der Sprenger (-)
watering can	die Gießkanne (n)
weedkiller	das Unkrautmittel (-)
fertilizer	Dünger (-)

Insects and pests *Insekten und Ungeziefer*

ant	die Ameise (n)
bee	die Biene (n)
greenfly	die Blattlaus (¨e)
housefly	die Hausfliege (n)
mosquito	die Stechmücke (n)
spider	die Spinne (n)
wasp	die Wespe (n)

Furniture, etc.

garden furniture	die Gartenmöbel
barbecue	der Gartengrill (s)
table	der Tisch (e)
deckchair	der Gartentisch (e)
lounger	der Liegestuhl (¨e)
bench	die Gartenbank (¨e)
swing	die Schaukel (n)
slide	die Rutsche (n)

Useful phrases

The grass needs to be cut.	Das Grass muss gemäht werden.
They are ripe/not ripe	Sie sind reif/noch nicht reif.
I like/dislike gardening.	Ich mag Gartenarbeit (nicht).
He/she has green fingers.	Er hat grüne Finger.
I am allergic to ...	Ich bin allergisch gegen ...
I have been stung!	Ich bin gestochen worden!

Useful verbs

to dig	<u>um</u>graben	*to water*	gießen
to plant	pflanzen	*to pick*	pflücken
to grow	wachsen	*to cut the grass*	schneiden
to weed	jäten		

Special plants and features

mixed woodland	der Mischwald
edelweiss	das Edelweiß
spruce	die Fichte (-n)
balcony box	der Balkonkasten (¨)

5.6 Tools and DIY

Core vocabulary

drill	die Bohrmaschine (n)
hammer	der Hammer (-)
pincers	die Kneifzange (n)
pliers	die Zange (n)
saw	die Säge (n)
chain saw	die Kettensäge (n)
screwdriver	der Schraubenzieher (-)
spanner	der Schraubenschlüssel (-)
tape measure	das Zentimetermaß (e)
nail	der Nagel (¨)
bolt	der Bolzen (-)
nut	die Schraube (-)
staple	die Krampe (n)
brush	die Bürste (n)
paint brush	die Farbbürste (n)
scissors	die Schere (n)

sandpaper	das Sandpapier (e)
ladder	die Leiter (n)
scaffold	das Gerüst (e)
tile	die Fliese (n)
slate	der Ziegelstein (e)
window frame	der Fensterrahmen (-)
shutters	der Fensterladen (¨)
pipe	das Rohr (e)
tap	der Hahn (¨e)
wire	der Draht (¨e)
fuse	die Sicherung (en)
plug	der Stecker (-)
socket	die Steckdose (n)

Useful words and phrases

Can you fix it?	Können Sie das reparieren?
Yes, I can!	Ja, das kann ich.
It is impossible/easy to fix.	Es ist unmöglich/einfach zu reparieren.
to fix something to a wall	etwas an der Wand befestigen
that does not work	das funktioniert nicht
it is broken	es ist kaputt
pull it up	heben Sie/heb es <u>hoch</u>
put it down	legen Sie/leg es <u>hin</u>
I have to try it out first.	Ich muss das erst <u>aus</u>probieren.
DIY	das Heimwerken
DIY shop (like B & Q)	Heimwerkergeschäft

Useful verbs

to screw	schrauben	*to rub down*	
to unscrew	<u>ab</u>schrauben	*(use sandpaper)*	schleifen
to hammer	hämmern	*to paint*	<u>an</u>streichen
to nail	nageln	*to plane*	hobeln
to drill	bohren	*to glue*	kleben
to fasten	befestigen	*to solder*	löten
to fix/mend	reparieren	*to weld*	schweißen
to cut	schneiden		

06

entertaining, food and drink

Parties and celebrations

re vocabulary

Congratulations!	Herzlichen Glückwunsch ...
on your birthday	zu Ihrem/deinem Geburtstag
on your anniversary	zum Jahrestag
on your engagement	zu Ihrer/eurer Verlobung
on your wedding	zur Hochzeit
on your silver wedding	zur Silberhochzeit
on your golden wedding	zur Goldenen Hochzeit
dinner	das Abendessen
a party	eine Party
a celebration	eine Feier

ℹ️ A formal invitation

We are pleased to announce the wedding of our daughter Anna with Mr Klaus Meier. The wedding ceremony takes place on Friday the 20th of October at 12 p.m. at St Magnus Church and afterwards lunch at Hotel Kaiser. We have great pleasure in inviting you.

Wir freuen uns die Hochzeit unserer Tochter Anna mit Herrn Klaus Meier bekannt zu geben. Die kirchliche Trauung findet am Freitag, dem 20.10. um 12 Uhr in der St. Magnus Kirche <u>statt</u>. Anschließend findet das Hochzeitsessen im Hotel Kaiser <u>statt</u>. Wir laden Sie dazu herzlich <u>ein</u>.

The reply

We thank you for your invitation to the marriage of your daughter and have great pleasure in accepting. Regards Mr and Mrs Braun

Vielen Dank für die Einladung zur Hochzeit Ihrer Tochter. Wir nehmen die Einladung gerne <u>an</u>. Mit freundlichen Grüßen Herr und Frau Braun

We very much regret that we are unable to accept the kind invitation but we will be attending a conference in America at that time.

Es tut uns außerordentlich Leid, dass wir Ihre freundliche Einladung nicht annehmen können, aber wir sind zu diesem Zeitpunkt auf einer Konferenz in Amerika.

An informal invitation

Can you come to a party at our house on Wed evening from 8 to 12?

Am Mittwochabend gebe ich von 8 Uhr bis 12 Uhr eine Party bei mir zuhause. Kannst Du kommen/Können Sie kommen?

We would be delighted to come and are looking forward to it very much.

Wir kommen sehr gerne und freuen uns schon darauf.

Excuses (Entschuldigungen)

Sorry we/I can't make it. **Es tut uns/mir Leid, wir können/ich kann da leider nicht.**

Unfortunately I have to go to … **Leider muss ich**

to Hamburg.	**nach Hamburg**
to the theatre.	**zum Theater**
to the university.	**zur Universität**

I will be away on business.	**Ich bin auf Geschäftsreise.**
on holiday.	**im Urlaub.**
I have a meeting that I can't get out of.	**Ich habe eine Besprechung, die ich leider nicht <u>ab</u>sagen kann.**
My mother is ill.	**Meine Mutter ist krank.**

More words

an invitation	eine Einladung
a reply	eine Antwort
an acceptance	eine Annahme
a refusal	eine Absage
an excuse	eine Entschuldigung
a thank you letter	ein Dankesschreiben
a cake	ein Kuchen
champagne	der Champagner/Sekt
a toast (e.g to the bride)	eine Ansprache/eine Trinkspruch
a present	ein Geschenk
cheers!	Zum Wohl/Prost

i You use **zum Wohl** when drinking champagne or wine and **Prost** in informal situations, mainly when drinking beer.

Useful phrases

Let's have a party.	Lassen Sie/Lass uns eine Party machen.
Let's dance.	Lassen Sie/lass uns tanzen.
I would like to propose a toast.	Ich möchte einen Trinkspruch machen.
I would like to thank our hosts.	Ich möchte dem/der Gastgeber/in danken.
I've got a hangover.	Ich habe einen Kater.
I can't drink, I am driving.	Ich kann nicht trinken, ich fahre Auto.
I don't drink alcohol.	Ich trinke keinen Alkohol.

Useful verbs

to *party*	feiern
to *eat*	essen
to *drink*	trinken
to *toast* (the bride)	<u>an</u>stoßen auf .../auf jemanden trinken
to *enjoy onseself*	sich amüsieren
to *overindulge/have too much*	es übertreiben, zu viel haben
to *get drunk*	betrunken werden
to *feel sick*	sich schlecht fühlen
to *be sober*	nüchtern sein
to *stay sober*	nüchtern bleiben

6.2 Eating out

Core vocabulary

restaurant	das Restaurant (s)
inn	das Gasthaus (¨er)
	die Gaststätte (n)
	die Wirtschaft (en)
café	das Café (s)
cake shop/café	die Konditorei (en)
icecream parlour	das Eiscafé (s)
snack bar	der Imbiss (e)
snack bar	die Imbissbude (n)
food stall	die Frittenbude (n)
beer garden	der Biergarten (¨)
pizzeria	die Pizzeria (ien)
bistro	das Bistro (s)
pub	die Kneipe (n)
bar	die Bar (s)

i The *dish of the day* is called **Menü** or **das Tagesmenü**, while the *menu* is **die Speisekarte**. A **Getränkekarte** is *various drinks*, while a **Weinkarte** is for *wine* only.

menu	die Speisekarte/die Karte (n)
wine list	die Weinkarte (n)
wine list	die Getränkekarte (n)
waiter	Ober/in
waiter	Kellner/in

service	die Bedienung
tip	das Trinkgeld (er)
bill	die Rechnung (en)
receipt	die Quittung (en)

i The best way to call a waiter/waitress is to say **Bedienung, bitte** (*service, please*). Avoid the expression **Fräulein**.

starter	die Vorspeise (n)
main course	die Hauptspeise (n)/das Hauptgericht (e)
dessert	der Nachtisch (-)/die Nachspeise (n)
coffee	der Kaffee

Useful phrases

Ich möchte ... bestellen	*I would like to order ...*
Ich hätte gerne ...	*I would like to ...*
Die Speisekarte/Getränkekarte bitte.	*The menu/wine list please.*
Ich möchte bezahlen.	*I would like to pay.*
Ist dieser Platz noch frei?	*Is this seat still free?*
nein, danke	*no thanks*
für Sie	*for you* (leaving a tip)
Es hat gut geschmeckt.	*It tasted very good.*

Useful verbs

to order	bestellen
to pay	bezahlen
to choose	auswählen
to taste	schmecken
to try	kosten/<u>aus</u>probieren
to take	nehmen
to book	bestellen
to reserve	reservieren
to take a seat	Platz nehmen
to serve	servieren

Drinks *Getränke*

soft drinks	alkoholfreie Getränke
orange juice	der Orangensaft (¨e)
water	das Wasser
mineral water	das Mineralwasser
fizzy	der Sprudel
still	ohne Kohlensäure
aperitif	der Aperitif (s)
cocktail	der Cocktail (s)
sherry	der Sherry (s)
gin and tonic	Gin und Tonic (s)
red wine	der Rotwein (e)
white wine	der Weißwein (e)
champagne	der Champagner (-)
brandy	der Brandy (s)
liqueur	der Likör (e)

6.3 German specialities

There are many dishes and specialities that are named after districts or cities:

Hamburger	*hamburger*
Frankfurter Bockwurst	*sausage from Frankfurt*
Königsberger Klopse	*meat balls in caper sauce*
Kieler Sprotten	*smoked sprats*
Rheinischer Sauerbraten	*marinated roast from Rhineland*
Thüringer Bratwurst	*grilled sausage*
Lübecker Marzipan	*marzipan from Lübeck*
Dresdener Christstollen	*traditional German Christmas cake from Dresden*
Schwarzwälder Kirschtorte	*Blackforest gateau*
Nürnberger Lebkuchen	*spiced biscuits from Franconia*
Bayrisches Sauerkraut	*Bavarian sauerkraut*

A lot of beers, too, are named after the area they come from:

Berliner Weiße	*beer shandy from Berlin*
Kölsch	*beer from Cologne*
Clausthaler	*beer from Clausthal*
Detmolder	*beer from Detmold*
Flensburger Weizen	*beer from Flensburg*

Germany is known for its sausages:

Bierwurst	*beer sausage*
Schinkenwurst	*ham sausage*
Fleischwurst	*meat sausage*
Geflügelwurst	*turkey sausage*
Leberwurst	*liver pate*
Salami	*salami*
Käsesalami	*cheese salami*
Pfeffersalami	*pepper salami*
Zwiebelsalami	*onion salami*
Kräutersalami	*herb salami*
Rohschinken	*smoked and air-dried hams*
gekochter Schinken	*cooked ham*
Bratwurst	*grilling sausage*
Knackwurst	*knackwurst*
Bockwurst	*bockwurst*
Cocktailwürstchen	*cocktail sausages*
Frankfurter	*frankfurter*

6.4 Fruit, vegetables and desserts

cauliflower	der Blumenkohl (e)
Brussels sprouts	der Rosenkohl (e)
red cabbage	der Rotkohl (e)
white cabbage	der Weisskohl(e)
peas	die Erbse (n)
green beans	die grünen Bohnen (-)
asparagus	der Spargel (-)
sauerkraut	das Sauerkraut
salad	der Salat (e)
cucumber	die Gurke (n)
lettuce	der Kopfsalat (e)
olives	die Oliven
radish	das Radieschen
spring onion	die Zwiebel (n)
tomato	die Tomate (n)
vegetables	das Gemüse
white beans	die weißen Bohnen
broccoli	der Brokkoli
cabbage	der Kohl/das Kraut
carrot	die Karotte (n)

courgette	die Zucchini (s)
garlic	der Knoblauch
leek	der Lauch
mushroom	der Pilz (e)
onion	die Zwiebel (n)
sweetcorn	der Mais
turnip	die Rübe (n)
shallots	die Schalotte (n)
spinach	der Spinat
cress	die Kresse
fruit	das Obst
apple	der Apfel (¨)
cooking apple	der Kochapfel
apricot	die Aprikose (n)
pineapple	die Ananas (-)
banana	die Banane (n)
grapes	die Weintrauben
cherry	die Kirsche (n)
melon	die Melone (n)
peach	der Pfirsich (e)
pear	die Birne (n)
plum	die Pflaume (n)
raspberry	die Himbeere (n)
rhubarb	der Rharbarba (-)
strawberry	die Erdbeere (n)
grapefruit	die Grapefruit (s), die Pampelmuse(n)
lemon	die Zitrone (n)
lime	die Limone (n)
orange	die Orange (n)
berries	die Beeren
blackcurrants	die schwarze Johannisbeere (n)
blueberry/bilberry	die Blaubeere (n)
cranberry	die Preiselbeere (n)
gooseberry	die Stachelbeere (n)
redcurrants	rote Johannesbeere (n)
avocado	die Avokado (s)
coconut	die Kokosnuss (¨e)
dates	die Dattel (n)
kiwi fruit	die Kiwi (s)
mango	die Mango (s)
passion fruit	die Passionsfrucht (¨e)
nuts	die Nuss (¨e)
almond	die Mandel (n)

cashew	die Cashewnuss ("e)
hazel	die Haselnuss ("e)
peanut	die Erdnuss ("e)
pistachio	die Pistazie (n)
walnut	die Walnuss ("e)
lentil	die Linse (n)
pumpkin	der Kürbis (se)
potato	die Kartoffel (n)
rice	der Reis (-)
pasta	die Nudeln (pl)
	die Spagetti (pl)
	Spätzle (type of pasta)
chips	die Pommes frites (pl)
dessert	die Nachspeise (n)
fruit sundae	der Früchtebecher (-)
chocolate gateau	die Sachertorte (n)
cheesecake	die Käsetorte (n)
apple strudel	der Apfelstrudel (-)
whipped cream	die Schlagsahne
ice cream	das Eis (-)
apricot	Aprikoseneis
strawberry	Erdbeereis
chocolate	Schokoladeneis
vanilla	Vanilleeis
coconut	Kokosnusseis
pistachio	Pistazieneis
lemon	Zitroneneis
raspberry	Himbeereis
gooseberry	Stachelbeereis
stracciatella	Stracciatella
vanilla with almonds	Vanilleeis mit Mandeln

i Germany is known for its *soft cheese* (**Quark**), eaten as a dessert with sweet ingredients such as fresh fruit:

cherries	**Kirschquark**
strawberries	**Erdbeerquark**
bananas	**Bananenquark**
apricot	**Aprikosenquark**
mixed fruit	**Früchtequark**

You can also eat **Quark** with savoury ingredients on bread, with *garlic* (**Knoblauch**) and *herbs* (**Kräutern**):

with herbs	**Kräuterquark**
with horseradish	**Mererettichquark**

6.5 Tea and coffee

Core vocabulary

coffee	der Kaffee
espresso	der Expresso
cappuccino	der Cappuccino
latte	der Milchkaffee
coffee with milk	Kaffee mit Milch
coffee without milk	schwarzer Kaffee
with sugar	mit Zucker
without sugar	ohne Zucker
with sweetener	mit Süßstoff
decaffeinated coffee	entkoffeinierter Kaffee
tea	der Tee
Indian tea	Indischer Tee
China tea	Chinesischer Tee
herbal tea	Kräutertee
peppermint tea	Pfefferminztee
camomile tea	Kamillentee
fruit tea	Früchtetee
green tea	Grüner Tee
ordinary tea	schwarzer Tee
with milk	mit Milch
with lemon	mit Zitrone
with sugar	mit Zucker
with honey	mit Honig

Useful phrases

I'm on a diet	Ich mache eine Diät
I am allergic to …	Ich bin allergisch gegen …
I don't eat …	Ich esse kein/e/n …
I can't eat …	Ich kann kein/e/n … essen
I am a vegan.	Ich bin Veganer/in.
I am a vegetarian.	Ich bin Vegetarier/in.
I am diabetic.	Ich bin Diabetiker/in.

Useful verbs

to like/dislike	mögen/nicht mögen
to eat	essen
to drink	trinken

to prefer	vorziehen
to love	lieben
don't like	nicht mögen
to hate	hassen
to do without	verzichten

6.6 Mealtimes

Core vocabulary

mealtimes	die Mahlzeiten
breakfast	das Frühstück
lunch	das Mittagessen
afternoon tea	Kaffee trinken
dinner	das Abendessen/Abendbrot
a snack	etwas Kaltes

ℹ Marmelade is not marmalade but jam. **Bittere Marmelade** is *marmalade*. It is very common to go to the bakery first thing in the morning to buy **frische Brötchen**, fresh warm crusty morning rolls.

Breakfast *das Frühstück*

wheat	der Weizen
oats	der Hafer
barley	die Gerste
rye	der Roggen
bran	die Kleie
cornflakes	die Kornflakes
muesli	das Müsli
milk	die Milch
semi-skimmed milk	die fettarme Milch
fat-free milk	die fettfreie Milch
soya milk	die Sojamilch
goat's milk	die Ziegenmilch
cream	die Sahne
yoghurt	der Joghurt (s)
bacon	der Speck
egg	das Ei (die Eier)
scrambled eggs	das Rührei
poached eggs	verlorene Eier
boiled egg	das gekochte Ei
hard boiled egg	das hartgekochte Ei
fried egg	das Spiegelei

sausages	die Wurst/Würstchen
tomatoes	die Tomaten
mushrooms	die Pilze
fried	gebraten
grilled	gegrillt
tinned	Dosen...
baked beans	gebackene weiße Bohnen
pancake	der Eierkuchen (-)/ Pfannkuchen (-)
maple syrup	der Ahornsirup
cooked ham	gekochter Schinken
cured ham	roher Schinken
salami	die Salami (s)
cheese	der Käse

Bread *das Brot*

white	das Weißbrot
brown	das Graubrot
farm bread	das Landbrot
farmer's loaf	das Bauernbrot (Switzerland)
granary	das Getreidebrot
wholemeal	das Vollkornbrot
organic	das Biobrot
pumpernickel	der Pumpernickel
rolls (crusty)	das Brötchen
rye bread	das Roggenbrot
sunflower bread	das Sonnenblumenbrot
croissants	die Croissants
linseed bread	das Leinsamenbrot
crispbread	das Knäckebrot
full grain rye bread	das Vollkornbrot
dark rye bread	das Schwarzbrot
sliced	geschnitten
butter	die Butter
margarine	die Margarine
low fat spread	fettarme Margarine
jam	die Marmelade
marmalade	bittere Marmelade
honey	der Honig

Drinks *die Getränke*

tea	der Tee (-)
coffee	der Kaffee
milk	die Milch
cold milk	die kalte Milch
hot milk	die heiße Milch
hot chocolate	die heiße Schokolade
fruit juice	der Fruchtsaft (¨e)
orange juice	der Orangensaft
freshly squeezed orange juice	frisch gepresster Orangensaft

(For more on coffees and teas, see page 130.)

Useful phrases

I don't eat breakfast.	Ich esse kein Frühstück.
I only eat …	Ich esse nur …
I don't drink milk …	Ich trinke keine Milch.
I have my breakfast at …	Ich esse Frühstück um … Uhr

6.7 Snacks

Core vocabulary

cheeseburger	der Cheeseburger (-)
hamburger	der Hamburger
fishburger	der Fischburger
fish	der Fisch
salad	der Salat
green salad	der grüne Salat
tomato salad	der Tomatensalat (e)
mixed salad	der gemischte Salat
potato salad	der Kartoffelsalat
yoghurt	der Joghurt (s)
biscuit	der Keks (e)
chocolate biscuit	der Schokoladenkeks (e)
piece of cake	ein Stück Kuchen
sweets	die Süßigkeiten
cigarettes	die Zigaretten (-)

sandwich	
in brown bread	auf Graubrot
in white bread	auf Weissbrot
in a roll	in einem Brötchen
with/without mayonnaise	mit/ohne Mayonnaise
salad dressing	Salatsoße
curried sausage with mayonnaise	Currywurst mit Mayo
curried sausage with ketchup	Currywurst mit Ketchup
fried sausage	Bratwurst
fried sausage with potato salad	Bratwurst mit Kartoffelsalat
rissole	Frikadellen
pancake with apple puree	Pfannkuchen mit Apfelmus
pasta	die Nudeln
spaghetti	die Spaghetti
lasagne	die Lasagne
pizza	die Pizza
kebab	das Kebab

Useful phrases

Can I offer you a cup of coffee?	Kann ich Ihnen/dir einen Kaffee <u>an</u>bieten?
How do you take it?	Wie nehmen Sie/nimmst du ihn?
With milk or without milk?	Mit oder ohne Milch?
Do you take sugar?	Nehmen Sie/nimmst du Zucker?
Have you got sweetener?	Haben Sie/hast du Süsstoff?
Would you like a biscuit?	Möchten Sie/möchtest du einen Keks?
Yes please.	Ja bitte./Ja gerne.
No thank you.	Nein danke./Nein vielen Dank.
I am on a diet.	Ich mache eine Diät.
I don't take …	Ich nehme kein/e/n …
It's too hot/cold/spicy.	Es ist zu heiß/kalt/scharf.
It isn't cooked properly.	Es ist nicht richtig gar gekocht.
It is delicious!	Es schmeckt ausgezeichnet!

6.8 Fish, meat and cheese

Core vocabulary

anchovy	die Sardelle (n)
cod	der Kabeljau (s)
haddock	der Schellfisch (e)
herring	der Hering (e)
mackerel	die Makrele (n)
plaice	die Scholle (n)
sardine	die Sardine (n)
skate	der Rochen
sole	die Seezunge (n)
tuna	der Tunfisch (e)
crab	die Krabbe (n)
langoustine	die Languste (n)
lobster	der Hummer (-)
mussels	die Muschel (n)
oyster	die Auster (n)
prawn	die Garnele (n)
trout	die Forelle (n)
salmon	der Lachs (-)
perch	der Barsch (e)
pike	der Hecht (e)
eel	der Aal (e)
hake	der Seehecht (e)
jellyfish	die Qualle (n)
octopus	der Tintenfisch (e)
squid	der Tintenfisch (e)
whiting	der Weißfisch (e)
meat	das Fleisch
beef	das Rindfleisch
lamb	das Lamm
pork	das Schweinefleisch
veal	das Kalbfleisch
ham	der Schinken
liver	die Leber
kidneys	die Niere (n)
poultry	das Geflügel
chicken	das Huhn ("er)
chicken	das Hühnchen
turkey	der Truthahn ("e)
duck	die Ente (n)

goose	die Gans (¨e)
game	das Federwild
grouse	das Moorhuhn (¨er)
hare	der Hase (n)
partridge	das Rebhuhn (¨er)
pheasant	der Fasan (e)
pigeon	die Taube (n)
rabbit	das Kaninchen
venison	das Wild
wild boar	der Eber

6.9 Using a recipe

Core vocabulary

making a cake	einen Kuchen machen
ingredients	die Zutaten
flour	das Mehl
baking powder	das Backpulver
yeast	die Hefe
potato flower	die Kartoffelstärke
sugar	der Zucker
butter	die Butter
salt	das Salz
melted chocolate	geschmolzene Schokolade
grated lemon rind	geriebene Zitronenschale
the juice of an orange	der Saft einer Orange
chopped nuts	gehackte Nüsse
grated chocolate	geriebene Schokolade
weighing scale	die Waage (n)
mixing bowl	die Schüssel (n)
wooden spoon	der Holzlöffel (-)
mixer	der Mixer (-)
grater	die Reibe (n)
sieve	das Sieb (e)
baking tin	die Backform (en)
oven	der Ofen (¨)
oven glove	der Ofenhandschuh (e)
silver foil	die Silberfolie
cling film	die Plastikfolie
plastic bags	die Plastiktüten
plastic containers	die Plastikdosen
saucepan	der Kochtopf (¨e)

casserole	die Kasserole (n)
frying pan	die Pfanne (n)
lid	der Deckel (-)
handle	der Griff (e)
making soup	eine Suppe machen
prepare the vegetables	das Gemüse <u>vor</u>bereiten
peel the carrots	die Mohrrüben schälen
chop the leeks	den Lauch hacken
melt the butter	die Butter schmelzen
add the flour	das Mehl <u>zu</u>geben
stir the mixture	die Mischung verrühren
pour in the stock	die Brühe <u>ein</u>gießen

Useful verbs

to heat	erwärmen
to cook	kochen
to roast	rösten
to bake	backen
to fry	braten
to boil	kochen
to poach	pochieren

i Bratkartoffeln mit Eiern und Petersilie

1 kg gekochte Pellkartoffeln
60 g Butter
2 große Zwiebeln
Salz
frisch gemahlener weißer Pfeffer
6 Eier
1/8 l Schlagsahne
1 EL gehackte Petersilie

Zubereitung: ca. 30 Minuten

Pellkartoffeln <u>ab</u>ziehen und in Scheiben schneiden. Butter in einer großen Pfanne erhitzen. Kartoffelscheiben darin goldbraun braten. Zwischendurch die geschälten, gewürfelten Zwiebeln zugeben, salzen und pfeffern. Eier mit Schlagsahne verquirlen. Petersilie <u>unter</u>heben. Auf die Bratkartoffeln gießen und stocken lassen.

Guten Appetit!

07

in town

7.1 Town plan and sights

Core vocabulary

bank	die Bank (en)
bus station	die Bushaltestelle (n)
car park	der Parkplatz (¨e)
cinema	das Kino (s)
football ground	der Fußballplatz (¨e)
hospital	das Krankenhaus (¨er)
hotel	das Hotel (s)
library	die Bücherei (en)
market	der Markt (¨e)
post office	das Postamt (¨er)
station	der Bahnhof (¨e)
swimming pool	das Schwimmbad (¨er)
tourist office	das Verkehrsbüro (s)
town hall	das Rathaus (¨er)
bridge	die Brücke (n)
castle	das Schloss (¨er)
cathedral	die Kathedrale (n)
church	die Kirche (n)
fountain	der Springbrunnen (-)
monument	das Denkmal (¨er)
museum	das Museum (Museen)
old town	die Altstadt (¨e)
opera house	das Opernhaus (¨er)
park	der Park (s)
river	der Fluss (¨e)
square	der Platz (¨e)
statue	die Statue (n)
theatre	das Theater (-)
region	die Region (en)
district	der Bezirk (e)
town	die Stadt (¨e)
suburb	der Stadtrand (¨er)
town centre	die Stadtmitte (n)
industrial zone	die Industriezone (n)
council offices	die Kommunalverwaltung
law court	das Gericht (e)
police station	die Polizeistation (en)
opening times	die Öffnungszeiten
open	geöffnet
closed	geschlossen

holidays	die Ferien
bank holiday	der Feiertag (e)
annual holiday	jährlicher Urlaub

Useful phrases

The town hall is situated on the square.	Das Rathaus befindet sich auf dem Platz.
We'll meet at the Kurfürstendamm.	Wir treffen was uns auf dem Kurfürstendamm.
Where is ...?	Wo ist ...?
It is in the centre.	Es ist im Stadtzentrum.
on the main street	an der Hauptstraße
near the post office	in der Nähe der Post
opposite the bank	gegenüber der Bank
at the marketplace	auf dem Marktplatz
beside the river	neben dem Fluss

Useful verbs

to meet	treffen
to look for	suchen
to be situated	gelegen sein
to be situated	sich befinden

i If you ring up to find out when the bank is open, this is the sort of message you might hear:

Unsere Bankfiliale ist montags von 8 Uhr bis 16 Uhr geöffnet. Wir sind samstags und sonntags geschlossen.
The bank is open Mondays from 8 a.m. to 4 p.m. We are closed on Saturdays and Sundays.

At a doctor's surgery.
Hier ist die Gemeindschaftpraxis von Dr. Sauer und Dr. Blumenstock. Es tut uns Leid, aber die Praxis ist zur Zeit geschlossen. Unsere Öffnungszeiten sind wie folgt: montags bis freitags von 9 Uhr bis 18 Uhr. In dringenden Notfällen rufen Sie bitte die folgende Telefonnummer an ...
You are connected to the surgery of Dr Sauer and Dr Blumenstock. We are sorry but our surgery is closed at present. Our opening hours are as follows: Monday to Friday from 9 a.m. to 6 p.m. In an emergency please phone the following telephone number ...

Core vocabulary

road/street	die Straße (n)
avenue	die Allee (n)
pavement	der Bürgersteig (e)
gutter	die Gosse (n)
pedestrian	der Fußgänger
pedestrian crossing	der Zebrastreifen (-)
pedestrian zone	die Fußgängerzone (n)
traffic lights	die Ampel (n)
subway (foot passage)	die Unterführung (en)
parking disc	die Parkscheibe
parking meter	die Parkuhr
How do I get into town?	Wie komme ich in die Stadt?
by car	mit dem Auto
by bus	mit dem Bus
by tram	mit der Straßenbahn
by subway (metro)	mit der U-Bahn
by bike	mit dem Fahrrad
Where is ...?	Wo ist ...?
the bus stop	die Bushaltestelle
the subway station	die U-Bahnstation
the taxi stop	der Taxistand
parking the car	das Auto parken
car park	der Parkplatz (¨e)
multi-storey car park	das Parkhaus (¨er)
underground car park	die unterirdische Garage
full	besetzt
spaces	frei
entrance	Eingang (¨e)
ticket machine	der Parkautomat (en)
change	das Wechselgeld
credit card	die Kreditkarte (n)
ticket	das Ticket(s)/die Karte (n)
exit	der Ausgang (¨e)
barrier	die Schranke (n)
traffic warden	der/die Verkehrspolizist/in (en) (nen)
one-way street	die Einbahnstraße (n)

ℹ️ Most car parks will have signs telling you how many spaces are available on each floor and some will even indicate which spaces are free:

Plätze frei	*free spaces*
voll	*no spaces*
besetzt	*no spaces*

Useful words and phrases

Cross the road.	Überqueren Sie/Überquer die Straße!
Use the crossing!	Benutzen Sie/Benutz den Übergang!
Don't cross!	Nicht überqueren!
There's a car coming!	Da kommt ein Auto!
Wait until it is green.	Warten Sie/warte bis es grün ist!
Go	Gehen Sie/geh
Excuse me ...	Entschuldigen Sie?/ Entschuldigung
Can you tell me ...	Können Sie mir sagen ...
How do I get to ...?	Wie komme ich zur/ zum/nach ...?
Where is the nearest car park?	Wo ist der nächste Parkplatz?
When is the next bus to ...?	Wann fährt der nächste Bus nach ...?

Useful verbs

to *walk*	gehen
to *cross*	überqueren
to *turn left/right*	rechts/links <u>ab</u>biegen
to *go straight on*	geradeaus gehen
to *run*	laufen
to *drive*	fahren
to *catch the bus*	einen Bus nehmen
to *miss the bus*	einen Bus verpassen

ℹ️ Some street signs you might see in pedestrian areas:

Kein Eintritt	*No entrance*
Notausgang	*Emergency exit*
Kein Trinkwasser	*Not drinking water*

Vorsicht!	*Danger!*
Links gehen	*Go to the left*
Haltestelle	*Bus/tram stop*
Vorsicht! Bauarbeiten	*Careful! Building work*
Achtung! Fahrradfahrer	*Careful! Cyclists*
	It is forbidden
Schwimmen verboten	*to swim*
Rauchen verboten	*to swim*
Rasen betreten verboten	*to walk on the grass*
Ball spielen verboten	*to play ball*

7.3 Shops and shopping

Core vocabulary

shop	das Geschäft /e
bakery	der Bäcker/ die Bäckerei (en)
butcher	der Fleischer/die Metzgerei (en)
cake shop	die Konditorei (en)
chemist	die Drogerie (n)
clothes shop	das Kleidungsgeschäft (e)
department store	das Kaufhaus (¨er)
flower shop	das Blumengeschäft (e)
hairdresser	der Frisör (e)
market	der Markt (¨e)
shoe shop	der Schuhladen (¨)
sports shop	das Sportgeschäft (e)
supermarket	der Supermarkt (¨e)
confectioner	der Süßwarenladen (¨)
sweetshop	das Süßigkeitsgeschäft (e)
shopping centre	das Einkaufszentrum (en)
hypermarket	großer Supermarkt (¨e)
department store	das Kaufhaus (¨er)
health food store	das Reformhaus (¨er)/der Naturkostladen (¨)
whole food shop	der Bioladen (¨)
newsagent	das Zeitungsgeschäft (e)
optician	der Optiker (-)
dry cleaners	die Reinigung (en)
travel agent	das Reisebüro (s)
escalator	die Rolltreppe (n)
lift	der Lift (s)/der Aufzug (¨e)/ der Fahrstuhl (¨e)

ground floor	das Erdgeschoss
first floor	der erste Stock/die erste Etage
bedding	die Bettwaren
department	die Abteilung (en)
fashion	die Modeabteilung (en)
sportswear	die Sportabteilung (en)
casualwear	die Freizeitkleidung
children's wear	die Kinderabteilung
leather goods	Lederwaren
television and electrical goods	Elektrobedarf
salesperson	der/die Verkäufer/in (-) (nen)
cash desk	die Kasse (n)
changing room	die Umkleidekabine (n)
customer, client	der/die Kunde/in
price	der Preis (e)
deposit	die Anzahlung (en)
discount	die Ermäßigung (en)

Useful phrases

How much does it cost?	Wie viel kostet es?
How are you paying?	Wie bezahlen Sie/bezahlst du?
Are you paying cash?	Bezahlen Sie bar?
Do you have the right change?	Haben Sie es passend?
Will you wrap it as a gift?	Können Sie es als Geschenk einpacken?
It is out of stock.	Wir haben es nicht auf Lager.

Useful verbs

to buy	kaufen	*to order*	bestellen
to sell	verkaufen	*to deliver*	liefern
to look for	suchen	*to window shop*	bummeln
to pay	bezahlen	*to choose*	aussuchen/auswählen
to prefer	bevorzugen	*to decide*	entscheiden
to go shopping	einkaufen		

The sales

der Sommerschlussverkauf	*summer sales*
der Sommer	*the summer*
der Schluss	*the end*

der Verkauf	*the sale*
der Winterschlussverkauf	*winter sales*
der Ausverkauf	*sales*
20% Ermäßigung	*20% reduction*
das Schnäppchen	*bargain*

7.4 At the supermarket

Core vocabulary

food department	die Lebensmittelabteilung (en)
fruit and vegetables department	Obst- und Gemüseabteilung (en)
dairy goods	Milchprodukte
frozen foods	Tiefkühlkost
cleaning materials	Reinigungsmittel
electrical goods	Elektroartikel
household appliances	Haushaltsgeräte
CDs	CDs
videos	Videos
wines and spirits	Wein und Spirituosen
drinks	Getränke
bottle of water	die Flasche (n) Wasser
jar of jam	die Dose (n) Marmelade
box of paper hankies	die Packung (en) Papiertücher
tin of tomatoes	die Dose Tomaten (n)
packet of biscuits	die Packung (en) Kekse
tube of toothpaste	die Tube (n) Zahnpasta
photographic shop	das Fotogeschäft (e)
dry cleaning	die Kleiderreinigung (en)
flower shop	der Blumenladen (-)
card shop	das Kartengeschäft (e)
shopping list	die Einkaufsliste (n)
coffee	der Kaffee (s)
tea bags	die Teebeutel (-)
yoghurt	der Joghurt (s)
juice	der Saft (¨e)
milk	die Milch
water	das Wasser
sugar	der Zucker
flour	das Mehl
rice	der Reis
pasta	die Nudeln
instant meals	die Fertiggerichte

microwaveable meals	Mikrowellenprodukte
detergent	Waschmittel (-)
for the washing machine	Waschmaschinenpulver (-)
for the dishwasher	der Geschirrspülmaschinen-reiniger (-)
for the washing up	das Geschirrspülmittel (-)
cleaner	der Reiniger (-)
for the kitchen	der Küchenreiniger (-)
for the bathroom	der Badezimmerreiniger (-)
for the toilet	der Toilettenreiniger (-)
for glass	das Glasreinigungsmittel (-)
stain remover	der Fleckenentferner (-)
polish	die Politur (en)
assistant	der/die Verkäufer/in (-) (nen)
basket	der Einkaufskorb (¨e)
trolley	der Einkaufswagen (-)
cash dispenser	der Geldautomat (en)
check out	die Kasse (n)

Useful phrases

Where is/are the …?	Wo gibt es …?
on the … aisle/shelf	im Gang/im Regal
Where is the gardening section?	Wo ist die Gartenabteilung?
on the row with the …	in dem Gang mit …
at the far end	am hinteren Ende
on the left/right-hand side	auf der linken/rechten Seite
Is there a restaurant?	Gibt es dort ein Restaurant?
What time do you shut?	Um wie viel Uhr schließen Sie?
Are you open on a Sunday?	Sind Sie sonntags geöffnet?

Useful verbs

to weigh	wiegen
to look for	suchen
to find	finden
to deliver	beliefern/liefern
to order	bestellen
to order in advance	in Voraus bestellen

7.5 At the post office and the bank

Core vocabulary

letter box	der Briefkasten (¨)
post office	die Post/das Postamt (¨er)
letter	der Brief (e)
packet	das Paket (e)
parcel	das Päckchen
postcard	die Postkarte (n)
writing paper	das Briefpapier
envelope	der Umschlag (¨e)
pen (ballpoint)	der Kugelschreiber (-)
stamp	die Briefmarke (n)
postman/woman	der/die Briefträger/in
money	das Geld
cash	das Bargeld
coins	die Münzen
notes	die Scheine
cheque book	das Scheckbuch (¨er)
credit card	die Kreditkarte (n)
phone card	die Telefonkarte (n)
telephone box	die Telefonzelle (n)
printed matter	die Drucksache (n)
recorded delivery	das Einschreiben (n)
overnight delivery	die Express-Lieferung (en)
air mail	die Luftpost
email	die E-Mail
cash machine	der Geldautomat (en)
cash transfer	die Geldüberweisung (en)
date	das Datum (die Daten)
amount	der Betrag (¨e)
signature	die Unterschrift (en)
sort code	die Bankleitzahl (en)
account number	die Kontonummer (n)
credit card number	die Kreditkartennummer (n)
expiry date	das Auslaufdatum (daten)
balance	der Kontostand
loan	der Kredit (e), das Darlehen (e)
mortgage	die Hypothek (en)

Useful words and phrases

insert your card	stecken Sie die Karte <u>ein</u>
type in your number	tippen Sie die Nummer
wait	warten Sie
remove your card	entfernen Sie Ihre Karte
take your money	nehmen Sie Ihr Geld
fill in the form	füllen Sie das Formular <u>aus</u>
go to the counter/cash desk	gehen Sie zum Schalter/zur Kasse
Where do I have to sign?	Wo muss ich <u>unter</u>schreiben?
How much does it cost to send this to …?	Wie viel kostet es, das nach … zu senden?
by air mail	per Luftpost

Useful verbs

Note that all the verbs in this section are *separable*.

to *withdraw cash*	Geld <u>ab</u>heben	to *sign*	<u>unter</u>schreiben
to *deposit*	<u>ein</u>bezahlen	to *fill in*	<u>aus</u>füllen
to *transfer*	<u>über</u>weisen	to *phone*	<u>an</u>rufen

Extras

der Brief	*letter*
der/die Briefträger/in	*postman/woman*
der Briefkasten	*post box*
der Briefmarkenautomat	*stamp machine*
der Briefumschlag	*envelope*
der Briefkopf	*letterhead*
die Briefdrucksache	*circular*
der/die Brieffreund/in (e) (nen)	*penfriend*
der Briefverkehr	*correspondence*
mit jemandem brieflich verkehren	*to correspond with somebody*
die Briefmarke auf den Brief kleben	*to stick the stamp on the letter*
den Brief in den Briefkasten stecken	*to put the letter in the letterbox*
elektronischer Briefkasten	*electronic mail box*

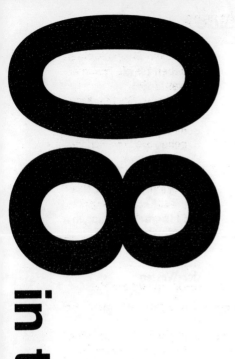

08

in the country

8.1 The countryside

Core vocabulary

in the countryside	auf dem Land
field	das Feld (er)
meadow	die Wiese (en)
footpath	der Fußweg (e)
hill	der Hügel (-)
mountain	der Berg (e)
stream	der Strom (¨e)
river	der Fluss (¨e)
lake	der See (n)
valley	das Tal (¨er)
points of the compass	die Himmelsrichtungen
north	der Norden
south	der Süden
east	der Osten
west	der Westen
northeast	der Nordosten
southwest	der Südwesten
northwest	der Nordwesten
southeast	der Südosten
grass	das Gras (¨er)
plant	die Pflanze (n)
wild flower	die Wildpflanze (n)
moss	das Moos (e)
mushroom	der Pilz (e)
fern	das Farn (e)
bush	der Busch (¨e)
tree	der Baum (¨e)
wood, forest	das Wald (¨er)
hedge	die Hecke (n)
fence	der Zaun (¨e)
ditch	das Gebüsch (e)
gate	das Tor (e)
spring	die Wasserquelle (n)
pond	der Brunnen (-)
bridge	die Brücke (n)
waterfall	der Wasserfall (¨e)
weir	das Stauwehr (e)
watermill	die Wassermühle (n)
reservoir	das Wasserreservoir (e)
dam	der Damm (¨e)

hydroelectric power station	das Elektrizitätswerk(e)
copse	das Wäldchen (-)
beech	die Buche (n)
chestnut	die Kastanie (n)
elm	die Ulme (n)
oak	die Eiche (n)
sycamore	der Bergahorn (e)
willow	die Weide (n)

Useful phrases

Where shall we go?	Wohin sollen wir gehen?
What shall we do?	Was sollen wir tun/machen?
How shall we go?	Wie sollen wir gehen?

Useful verbs

to go for a walk	spazieren gehen
to go swimming	schwimmen gehen
to go hiking	wandern (gehen)
to ride a bike	Fahrrad fahren
to go fishing	fischen (gehen)

8.2 In the mountains

Core vocabulary

hill	der Hügel (-)
mountain	der Berg (e)
mountain range	die Bergkette (n)
mountain pass	der Bergpass (¨e)
mountain path	der Bergweg (e)
mountain railway	die Bergbahn (en)
elevated railway	die Schwebebahn (en)
funicular railway	die Drahtseilbahn (en)
mountain hut/refuge	die Berghütte (n)
cable car	die Gondelbahn (en)
summit	der Gipfel (-)
the weather	das Wetter
cloudy	wolkig
rainy	regnerisch
sunny	sonnig

dry	trocken
windy	windig
easy	leicht
moderately difficult	ziemlich schwierig
difficult	schwierig
extreme	extrem
peak	der Gipfel (-)
rock face	die Felswand (¨e)
slope	der Abhang (¨e)/das Gefälle (-)
gorge	die Schlucht (en)
cave	die Höhle (n)
equipment	die Ausrüstung (en)
rope	das Seil (e)
harness	der Klettergurt (e)
carabiner	der Karabiner (-)
rucksack	der Rucksack (¨e)
torch	die Taschenlampe (n)
stove	der Kocher (-)
dried food	getrocknetes Essen
waterproofs	wasserfeste Kleidung
knife	das Messer (-)
water bottle	die Wasserflasche (n)
sleeping bag	der Schlafsack (¨e)
tent	das Zelt (e)

Useful phrases

What is the forecast?	Wie ist die Wettervorhersage?
How difficult is it?	Wie schwierig ist es?
How long does it take?	Wie lange dauert es?

Useful verbs

to climb	klettern	*to hike*	wandern
to abseil	<u>ab</u>seilen	*to rock climb*	klettern
to bivouac	biwakieren		

8.3 At the seaside

Core vocabulary

seaside	an der See	sand	der Sand
sea	die See	sand dune	die Sanddühne (n)
ocean	der Ozean (e)	cliff	die Klippe (n)
wave	die Welle (n)	pebbles	die Steine
harbour	der Hafen (¨)	rock	der Felsen (-)
port	der Fährhafen (¨)	island	die Insel (n)
beach	der Strand (¨e)		

quay	der Kai (s)
reef	das Riff (e)
jetty	der Anlegesteg (e)/die Landungsbrücke (en)
pier	der Brückenpfeiler (-)
surf	die Brandung (en)
shore	die Küste (n)/das Ufer (-)
estuary	die Mündung (en)
cape, promontory	das Kap (s)
peninsula	die Halbinsel (n)
rowing boat	das Ruderboot (e)
yacht	die Yacht (en)
dinghy	das Schlauchboot (e)
motor boat	das Motorboot (e)
ferry boat	die Fähre (n)
car ferry	die Autofähre (n)
cruiser	das Kreuzfahrtsschiff (e)
liner	das Fahrgastschiff (e)
pilot	der Pilot (en)
sailing boat	das Segelboot (e)
navigation	die Navigation
port	der Backbord (-)
buoy	die Boje (n)
light house	der Leuchtturm (¨e)
boat	das Boot (e)
mast	der Mast (en)
sail	das Segel (-)
rudder	das Ruder (-)
anchor	der Anker (-)
satellite positioning	die Satellitenausrichtung (en)
automatic pilot	die automatische Ansteuerung (en)
ropes	die Seile
pedalboat	das Tretboot (e)

high tide	die Flut (en)
low tide	die Ebbe (n)
sea-level	der Meeresspiegel
calm	ruhig
choppy	böig
rough	rauh
sandy	sandig
rocky	felsig
smooth	ruhig

Useful phrases

When is high tide?	Wann ist Flut?
Where can I moor?	Wo kann ich mein Schiff <u>fest</u>machen?
We would like to hire a pedal boot.	Wir möchten gerne ein Tretboot mieten.

Useful verbs

to row	rudern	*to cast off*	<u>aus</u>werfen
to sail	segeln	*to tie up*	<u>an</u>binden
to motor	mit Motor fahren		

8.4 Working in the countryside

Core vocabulary

agriculture	die Landwirtschaft/die Agrarindustrie
bee keeping	die Bienenzucht
game keeping	die Wildhaltung
horticulture	der Gartenbau
wine growing	der Weinbau
forestry	das Forstwesen, die Forstwirtschaft
tractor	der Traktor (en)
trailer	der Anhänger (-)
plough	der Pflug (¨e)
harvester	die Erntemaschine (n)
farm	die Farm (en)

market	der Markt (¨e)
garden	der Garten (¨)
farmhouse	das Bauernhaus (¨er)
barn	die Scheune (n)
stable	der Stall (¨e)
cattle shed	der Rinderschuppen (-)
crops	die Ernte (n)
grain	das Getreide
barley	die Gerste
oats	der Hafer
rice	der Reis
rye	der Roggen
wheat	der Weizen
hay	das Heu
straw	das Stroh
farmshop	der Bauernladen (¨)
bee keeper	der/die Imker/in, Bienenzüchter/in (-) (nen)
farmer	der/die Bauer/in (-) (nen)
farm worker	der/die Landarbeiter/in (-) (en)
horticulturalist	der/die Gärtner/in (-) (en)
vet	der/die Tierarzt (¨e)/in (en)
wine grower	der/die Weinbauer/in (-) (en)
vineyard	der Weinberg (e)
vine	die Rebe (-)
grape	die Weintraube (n)
fruit growing	der Obstbau
apples	Äpfel
cherries	Kirschen
poultry	das Federvieh
turkey	der Truthahn (¨e)
pheasant	der Fasan (e)

Words for families of animals

cow die Kuh (¨e)	*heifer* die junge Kuh (¨e)	*bull* der Bulle (n)	*calf* das Kalb (¨er)
sheep das Schaf (e)	*ewe* das Mutterschaf (e)	*ram* der Bock (¨e)	*lamb* das Lamm (¨er)
sow die Sau	*pig* das Schwein (e)	*boar* der Eber (-)	*piglet* das Schweinchen
goat die Ziege (-)	*nanny* die Zicke (-)	*billy kid* der Ziegenbock (¨e)	

dog	bitch	puppy
der Hund (e)	die Hündin (en)	kleine(r) Hund (e)/Hündchen (-)
hen	chicken	
die Henne (n)	das Hühnchen	
duck	duckling	
die Ente (n)	das Entlein	
goose	gosling	
die Gans (¨e)	das Gänschen	

Useful phrases

Beware of the dog!	Vorsicht! Hund
Please shut the gate	Tor schließen bitte
electric fence	elektrischer Zaun
No entry/entrance	kein Eintritt

Useful verbs

to *cultivate*	kultivieren
to *plant*	pflanzen
to *spread fertilizer*	düngen
to *weed*	Unkraut jäten
to *harvest*	ernten
to *feed*	füttern
to *milk*	melken
to *breed*	züchten
to *sow*	sähen
to *pick*	pflücken
to *take to market*	zum Markt bringen

ℹ️ tägliche Weinproben	*daily wine tasting*
Bauernkäse	*farmhouse cheese*
Schafskäse	*goat's cheese*
Spargel stechen	*PYO asparagus*
frische Erdbeeren	*fresh strawberries*
frische Landeier	*fresh country eggs*

09

hobbies and sports

9.1 Hobbies

Core vocabulary

I like ...	ich ... gerne/ich mag ...
I like to jog	ich jogge gerne
I like jazz dance	ich mag Jazztanz
acting	schauspielern
cooking	kochen
dancing	tanzen
modern	moderne Tänze
ballroom	Standardtänze
DIY	heimwerkern
drawing	zeichnen
gardening	die Gartenarbeit
going out (socially)	<u>aus</u>gehen
horse riding	reiten
listening to music	Musik hören
meeting people	Leute treffen
painting	malen
photography	fotografieren
playing tennis	Tennis spielen
playing football	Fußball spielen
to do pottery	töpfern
reading	lesen
sailing	segeln
sewing	schneidern
singing	singen
sport	Sport treiben/machen
walking	spazieren gehen
watching films	Filme <u>an</u>sehen
watching television	<u>fern</u>sehen
writing	schreiben
birdwatching	Vögel beobachten
fishing	fischen
hunting	jagen
shooting	schießen
rambling	wandern (gehen)

Useful words and phrases

archaeology	die Archäologie
astronomy	die Astronomie
history	die Geschichte

historical sites	historische Plätze
touring	Reisen/Touren machen
visiting foreign countries	ferne Länder besuchen
playing chess/cards/ bridge/party games	Schach/Karten/ Bridge/Partyspiele spielen
bingo	Bingo
jigsaw puzzle	Puzzle
dominoes	Domino
draughts	Dame
billiards	Billard
snooker	Snooker
table football	Tischfußball
crossword	Kreuzworträtsel
making music	Musik machen
playing in an orchestra	im Orchester spielen
singing in a group	in einer Gruppe singen
playing an instrument	ein Instrument spielen
piano	das Klavier
guitar	die Gitarre
violin	die Violine
trumpet	die Trompete
drums	die Trommel
What do you do in your free time?	Was machen Sie/machst du in Ihrer/deiner Freizeit?
Do you like ...?	Mögen Sie/magst du ...?
I like meeting people.	Ich treffe gerne Leute.
I do (painting).	Ich male.
I belong to a club.	Ich gehöre einem Club an.
We meet every week, month.	Wir treffen jede Woche, jeden Monat.
It's interesting/fantastic/ boring.	Es ist interessant/fantastisch/ langweilig.
I am interested in ...	Ich interessiere mich für ...

Useful verbs

to attend	teilnehmen
to be a member of	ein Mitglied sein
to be interested in	interessiert sein an
to be keen on	sich begeistern für
to enjoy	genießen
to meet	treffen
to spend my time	meine Zeit verbringen mit

9.2 Sports

Core vocabulary

ball game	das Ballspiel (e)
football	der Fußball
ball	der Ball (¨e)
team	das Team (s)
goal	das Tor (e)
match	das Spiel (e)
football ground	das Fußballfeld (er)
to score a goal	ein Tor schießen
rugby	das Rugby
player	der Spieler (-)
pitch	das Feld (er)
basketball	das Basketballspiel
basket	der Korb (¨e)
volleyball	das Volleyballspiel
net	das Netz
hockey	das Hockey
hockey stick	der Hockeyschläger
golf	das Golf
golf ball	der Golfball (¨e)
golf clubs	die Schläger
golf course	der Golfplatz (¨e)
green	das Grün (s)
hole	das Loch (¨er)
bunker	der Bunker (-)
clubhouse	das Clubhaus (¨er)
tee	das Tee (s)
to putt	putten
to hole a putt	einlochen
good putt	der gute Schlag (¨e)
tennis	das Tennisspiel (e)
tennis racquet	der Tennisschläger (-)
tennis court	der Tennisplatz (¨e)
tennis ball	der Tennisball (¨e)
tennis player	der Tennisspieler (-)
match	das Tennisspiel
doubles	das Doppel
singles	das Einzel
mixed doubles	das gemischte Doppel
service	der Aufschlag
love	null
set	der Satz

advantage	Vorteil
badminton	das Federballspiel (e)
net	das Federballnetz (e)
shuttlecock	der Federball (¨e)
squash	das Squash
squash court	der Squashcourt (s)
squash racquet	der Squashschläger (-)
boxing	das Boxen
judo	das Judo
karate	das Karate
tae-kwando	das Tae-kwando
wrestling	das Ringen
running	das Laufen
cross-country running	das Querfeldeinrennen
jumping	das Springen
hurdles	das Hürdenspringen
track	die Rennbahn (en)
aerobics	das Aerobic
gymnastics	die Gymnastik
jogging	das Joggen
weightlifting	das Gewichtheben
weight training	das Gewichtstraining
yoga	das Yoga

Useful phrases

I like ...	Ich mag/ich ... gerne
Do you like ...?	Mögen sie/Magst du ...?

Useful verbs

to win	gewinnen	*to box*	boxen
to lose	verlieren	*to do*	machen
to draw	unentschieden	*to jog*	joggen
a match	spielen	*to run*	rennen

9.3 More sports

Core vocabulary

water sports	der Wassersport
canoeing	Kanu fahren
canoe	das Kanu (s)

paddle	das Paddel (-)
diving (deep sea)	das Tiefseetauchen
wet suit	der Taucheranzug (¨e)
dry suit	der Trockenanzug (¨e)
oxygen cylinder	die Sauerstoffflasche (n)
mask	die Tauchermaske (n)
flippers	die Schwimmflossen (-)
snorkel	der Schnorchel (-)
rowing	das Rudern
boat	das Boot (e)
oar	das Ruder (-)
sailing	das Segeln
sail	das Segel (-)
surfing	das Surfen
surfboard	das Surfbrett (er)
wind surfing	das Windsurfen
wind surfer	der Windsurfer (-)
yachting	Boot fahren
yacht	die Yacht (en)
dinghy	das Schlauchboot (e)
swimming	das Schwimmen
breast stroke	das Brustschwimmen
front crawl	das Kraulen
butterfly	der Schmetterlingsstil
backstroke	das Rückenschwimmen
diving	das Tauchen
swimming pool	das Schwimmbecken (-)
length	die Länge (n)
diving board	das Sprungbrett (er)
swimming costume	der Schwimmanzug (¨e)
swimming trunks	die Badehose(n)
goggles	die Taucherbrille (n)
archery	das Bogenschießen
bow	der Bogen (-)
arrow	der Pfeil (e)
cycling	das Radfahren
racing bike	das Rennrad (¨er)
mountain bike	das Mountainbike(s)
bike	das Fahrrad (¨er)
handlebars	die Lenkstange (n)
saddle	der Sattel (-)
saddle bag	die Satteltasche (n)
fencing	das Fechten
foil	das Florett (s)

horse riding	das Reiten
saddle	der Sattel (-)
bridle	der Zaum (¨e)
stirrups	der Steigbügel (-)
roller skating	das Rollschuhlaufen
skates	die Rollschuhe
skateboarding	das Skaten
skateboard	das Skateboard (s)
climbing	das Klettern
mountain walking	das Bergwandern
mountaineering	das Bergsteigen
rock climbing	im Fels klettern
climbing boots	der Kletterschuh (e)
rope	das Kletterseil (e)
carabiner	der Karabiner (-)
rucksack	der Rucksack (¨e)
skiing	das Skifahren
skis	die Skier
poles	der Skistock (¨e)
piste	die Piste (n)
snowboarding	das Snowboarden
snowboard	das Snowboard (s)
sledging	das Schlittenfahren
sled	der Schlitten (-)
tobogganing	das Rodeln
toboggan	der Rodelschlitten (-)
ice skating	das Eislaufen
skates	die Schlittschuhe (-)
ice rink	der Eisring (e)

Useful phrases

I enjoy doing …	ich genieße …
I am good/not good at …	ich bin gut im …
I am good at …/I play … well	ich spiele gut/sehr gut …
I play regularly …	ich spiele regelmäßig …
I play from time to time …	ich spiele gelegentlich …
whenever I have time I …	so oft ich Zeit habe mache ich …

10

clothing

10.1 Garments and styles

Core vocabulary

clothes	die Kleidung
ladies fashion	die Damenbekleidung
blouse	die Bluse (n)
cardigan	die Strickjacke (n)
dress	das Kleid (er)
evening dress	das Abendkleid (er)
summer dress	das Sommerkleid (er)
jacket	die Jacke (n)
long jacket	die lange Jacke (n)
short jacket	die kurze Jacke (n)
jersey	der Pulli (s)
shorts	die Shorts
skirt	der Rock (¨e)
suit	der Anzug (¨e)
suit (jacket and skirt)	das Kostüm (e)
trouser suit	der Hosenanzug (¨e)
trousers	die Hose (n)
lingerie	die Damenunterwäsche
bra	der BH (s) (Büstenhalter)
knickers	die Unterhose (n)
slip	der Slip (s)
stocking/s	der Strumpf (¨)e
tights	die Strumpfhose (n)
nightie	das Nachthemd (en)
pyjamas	der Pyjama (s)
negligee	das Neglige (s)/das Hauskleid (er)/der Morgenanzug (¨e)
men's fashion	die Herrenmode
blazer	der Blazer (-)
jacket	das Jackett (s)
dinner jacket	der Smoking (s)
jeans	die Jeans (-)
jumper/pullover	der Pullover (-)
shirt	das Hemd (en)
shorts	die Shorts
socks	die Socken
suit	der Anzug (¨e)
sweatshirt	das Sweatshirt (s)
T-shirt	das T-shirt (s)
tie	die Krawatte (n)

trousers	die Hose (n)
belt	der Gürtel (-)
braces	die Hosenträger
waistcoat	die Weste (n)
boxer shorts	die Boxershorts
vest	das Unterhemd (en)
pyjamas	der Pyjama (s)/der Schlafanzug (¨e)
changing room	die Umkleidekabine
fitting room	der Anproberaum

i **Der Pyjama** is singular. **Die Hose** is singular. **Die Brille** is singular.

coat	der Mantel (¨)
raincoat	der Regenmantel (¨)
hat	der Hut (¨e)
scarf	der Schal (s)
gloves	die Handschuhe (-)

Useful phrases

The blue dress fits me.	Das blaue Kleid passt mir.
The hat suits me well.	Der Hut steht mir gut.
I will be wearing …	Ich werde eine/n … tragen
a dark suit	einen dunklen Anzug
a coat and hat	einen Mantel und einen Hut
a sweatshirt, jeans and trainers	ein Sweatshirt, Jeans und Turnschuhe
What will you be wearing?	Was werden Sie/wirst du tragen?
What size are you?	Welche Größe haben Sie/ hast du?
I wear size 10.	Ich trage Größe 10.
it is too short	es ist zu kurz
too wide	zu weit
too long	zu lang
too tight	zu eng
Have you got anything bigger/smaller?	Haben Sie es/ihn/sie etwas größer/kleiner?
in a different colour?	in einer anderen Farbe?
It suits you/It doesn't suit you.	Es steht Ihnen/dir gut/es steht Ihnen/dir nicht gut.

| I am going to wear a brown coat. | Ich ziehe einen braunen Mantel an. |
| Are you going to wear a dress or a skirt? | Ziehen Sie ein Kleid oder einen Rock an? |

i Notices you might find in a clothing department:

fehlerhaft	*faulty*
heruntergesetzte Kleidung	*reduced clothes*
reduziert	*reduced*
Größen 10–16	*sizes 10–16*
Übergrößen	*outsizes*
Umkleidekabine/raum	*changing room*

Useful verbs

to wear	tragen
to fit	passen
to suit	gut stehen
to get dressed	anziehen
to take off	ausziehen
to take off	ablegen
to get dressed	sich anziehen
to get undressed	sich ausziehen
to put on	überziehen
to get changed	sich umziehen/umkleiden
to try on	anprobieren

10.2 Measurements and materials

Core vocabulary

measurements	die Maße
tape measure	das Zentimetermaß (e)
length	die Länge (n)
width	die Weite (n)
size	die Größe (n)
collar	der Kragen (-)
neck	der Hals (¨e)
shoulders	die Schultern
sleeves	der Ärmel (-)
chest	der Brustumfang (¨e)
waist	die Taillenweite (n)

cuffs	die Manschette (-)
material	das Material (ien)
fabric	der Stoff (e)
It is made out of ...	Es ist aus ... gemacht
cotton	die Baumwolle
fur	der Pelz (-e)
artificial fur	künstlicher Pelz
jersey	der Jersey
leather	das Leder
linen	das Leinen
satin	der Satin
silk	die Seide
suede	das Wildleder
synthetic fibre	die Kunstfaser/die Chemiefaser
tweed	der Tweed
velvet	der Samt
wool	die Wolle
floral	geblümt
pleated	gefaltet
multi-coloured	mehrfarbig
patterned	gemustert
plain (one colour)	einfarbig
spotted	gepunktet
striped	gestreift
tartan	kariert
button	der Knopf (¨e)
cotton	der Faden (¨)
snap fastener	der Druckknopf (¨e)
needle	die Nadel (-n)
ribbon	die Schleife (n)
scissors	die Schere (n)
sewing machine	die Nähmaschine (n)
velcro	der Klettverschluss (¨e)
zip	der Reißverschluss (¨e)
detergent	das Waschmittel (-)
detergent for wool	Feinwaschmittel für Wolle
fabric softener	das Weichspülmittel (-)
soap powder	das Waschpulver (-)

Useful phrases

I have lost a button.	Ich habe einen Knopf verloren.
Can I get this dry cleaned/ pressed (ironed)?	Kann ich das gereinigt/ gebügelt bekommen?
How long will it take?	Wie lange dauert es?
Can you remove this stain?	Können Sie den Fleck entfernen?
Can you sew this button on?	Können Sie den Knopf annähen?
When do you need it back?	Wann möchten Sie es zurück haben?
Can you shorten it?	Können Sie es kürzen?
This garment must be dry cleaned.	Das Teil muss gereinigt werden.
This garment can be machine washed.	Das Teil ist waschmaschinenfest.
handwash only	nur Handwäsche
Don't use bleach.	Nicht bleichen.

Useful verbs

to wash	waschen
to dry	trocken
to dry clean	reinigen
to iron	bügeln
to mend	ändern

10.3 Special occasions

Core vocabulary

going to work	zur Arbeit gehen
uniform	die Uniform (en)
apron	die Schürze (n)
overall	der Kittel (-)
raincoat	der Regenmantel (¨)
rainhat	der Regenhut (¨e)
waterproof trousers	die wasserdichte Hose
rubber boots	die Gummistiefel
umbrella	der Schirm (e)/der Regenschirm (e)

anorak	der Anorak (s)
walking boots	die Wanderschuhe
thick socks	dicke Socken
woolly hat	die Wollmütze (n)
gloves	die Handschuhe
hard hat	der Schutzhelm (-e)
blue overalls	der blaue Overall
swimming costume	der Schwimmanzug (¨e)/der Badeanzug (¨e)
bikini	der Bikini (s)
trunks	die Badehose (n)
flippers	die Schwimmflossen
goggles	die Schwimmbrille (n)
snorkel	der Schnorchel (-)
flip flops	die Badelatschen/schuhe
suntan cream	die Sonnencreme (s)
evening wear	die Abendkleidung
evening dress	das Abendkleid (er)
high heels	die Stöckelschuhe
smart clothes	schicke Kleidung
polo shirt	das Polohemd (en)
shorts	die Shorts
socks	die Socken
trainers	die Turnschuhe
sweatshirt	das Sweatshirt (s)
T-shirt	das T-Shirt (s)
formal dress	die Gesellschaftskleidung
casual dress	die Freizeitkleidung
sports clothes	die Sportkleidung
school clothes	die Schulkleidung
jewellery	der Schmuck
bracelet	das Armband (¨er)
brooch	die Brosche (n)
earring	der Ohrring (e)
necklace	die Halskette (n)
ring	der Ring (e)
watch	die Uhr (en)
silver	das Silber
gold	das Gold
platinum	das Platin
diamond	der Diamant (en)
emerald	der Smaragd (e)
ruby	der Rubin (e)
sapphire	der Saphir (e)
semi-precious stone	der Halbedelstein (e)

Useful phrases

he/she always looks ...		er/sie sieht immer ... <u>aus</u>	
casual		leger	
elegant		elegant/vornehm	
fashionable		modisch	
smart		schick	
unfashionable		altmodisch	
untidy		unordentlich	
stylish		stilvoll	
to go out in		zum Ausgehen	
smart clothes to go out with		die Ausgehkleidung	
clothes	die Kleidung	cupboard	der Kleiderschrank (˙e)
to dress	sich kleiden	coat hanger	der Kleiderbügel (-)
flattering	schmeichel- haft	clothes on offer	das Kleidungs- angebot (e)
clothes department		die Kleidungsabteilung (en)	
dress regulations		die Kleiderordnung/zwang	

Useful verbs

to *wear*	tragen
to *take* off	<u>ab</u>legen
to *get dressed*	sich <u>an</u>ziehen
to *get undressed*	sich <u>aus</u>ziehen
to *put around*	<u>um</u>legen
to *put on*	<u>auf</u>setzen

10.4 Footwear

Core vocabulary

the shoe shop	das Schuhgeschäft (e)
hosiery	die Strumpfwaren
socks	die Socken
stockings	die Strümpfe
tights	die Strumpfhosen
leggings	die Leggings
I would like a pair of ...	Ich hätte gerne ein Paar ...
boots	Stiefel
clogs	Clogs
flip flops	Badelatschen
high heels	Stöckelschuhe

flat shoes	flache Schuhe
sandals	Sandalen
shoes	Schuhe
slip-ons	Schlipper
slippers	Pantoffeln/Hausschuhe
trainers	Turnschuhe
wellingtons/rubber boots	Gummistiefel
sport shoes	Sportschuhe
ballet shoes	Ballettschuhe
climbing boots	Kletterschuhe
cycling shoes	Fahrradschuhe
dancing shoes	Tanzschuhe
diving boots	Taucherflossen
flippers	Schwimmflossen
football boots	Fußballschuhe
golf shoes	Golfschuhe
ski boots	Skistiefel
tennis shoes	Tennisschuhe
walking boots	Wanderschuhe

leather	das Leder
rubber	das Gummi
synthetics	die Kunstfaser
shoe polish	die Schuhcreme
shoe cleaner	der Schuhreiniger (-)
shoe protector	der Schuhschoner (-)
shoe stretcher	der Schuhspanner (-)
chiropody	die Fußpflege
massage	die Massage (n)
reflexology	die Reflexologie
foot	der Fuß ("e)
toe	der Zeh (en)
ankle	das Fußgelenk (e)
sole	die Fußsohle (n)
toe nails	der Fußnagel (")
arch of the foot	der Spann

Useful words and phrases

barefoot	barfuß
I have got sore feet.	Mir tun die Füße weh.
I have got blisters.	Ich habe Blasen.
Have you got a plaster?	Haben Sie/hast du ein Pflaster?
What shoe size are you?	Was ist Ihre/deine Schuhgröße?
These shoes are comfortable/ uncomfortable.	Diese Schuhe sind bequem/ unbequem.

Useful verbs

to try shoes on	Schuhe anprobieren
to put on your shoes	Schuhe anziehen
to take off your shoes	Schuhe ausziehen
to get blisters	Blasen bekommen

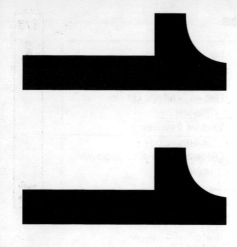

travel

11.1 Travel

Core vocabulary

journey	die Reise (n)
itinerary	der Reiseplan (¨e)
route	die Reiseroute (n)
map	die Landkarte (n)
overland	auf dem Landweg
by air	auf dem Luftweg
by sea	auf dem Seeweg
by public transport	mit öffentlichen Verkehrsmitteln
by train	mit dem Zug
by plane	mit dem Flugzeug
by coach	mit dem Bus
by car	mit dem Auto
by hire car	mit dem gemieteten Auto
by boat	mit dem Boot
by ferry	mit der Fähre
by bike	mit dem Fahrrad
on horseback	zu Pferd
on foot	zu Fuß
timetable	der Fahrplan (¨e)
ticket (train, bus, tram)	das Ticket (s)/die Fahrkarte (n)
ticket (plane)	der Flugschein (e)/das Ticket(s)
booking, reservation	die Buchung (en)/die Reservierung (en)
online booking	die Online-Buchung (en)
arrival	die Ankunft (¨e)
departure (train, bus)	die Abfahrt (en)
departure (plane)	der Abflug (¨e)

Useful phrases

Can you help me please?	Können Sie mir bitte helfen?
I'm lost ...	Ich habe mich verlaufen ...
How do I get to ...?	Wie komme ich zum/zur ...
Is it far (to ...)?	Ist es weit (zum/zur ...)?
How far is it?	Wie weit ist es?
How long does it take?	Wie lange dauert das?

| *Where is the next bus stop?* | Wo ist die nächste Bushaltestelle? |
| *What is the best way to go to ...?* | Wie komme ich am besten zum/zur ...? |

Useful verbs

to travel	reisen
to go	fahren
to sail	segeln
to fly	fliegen
to drive	fahren
to tour	touren
to arrive	<u>an</u>kommen
to leave	<u>ab</u>fahren

i You use **zum** for masculine and neuter nouns and **zur** for feminine nouns:

Wie komme ich *zum* Bahnhof? (m)
Wie komme ich *zum* Theater? (n)
Wie komme ich *zur* Tankstelle? (f)

i Remember to use **fahren** when travelling by bus, train, car or even bicycle:

Ich fahre mit dem Fahrrad.
Ich fahre mit dem Bus in den Harz.
I *go* to Austria. Ich **fahre** nach Österreich.

Other words and phrases with *fahren*

<u>hin</u>fahren	*to go to*
<u>zurück</u>fahren	*to go back*
den Berg <u>hoch</u>fahren	*to go up the hill*
den Berg <u>runter</u>fahren	*to go down the hill*
geradeaus fahren	*to go straight on*
in die Einbahnstraße fahren	*to go into a one-way street*
<u>weiter</u>fahren	*to continue driving*
Fahren Sie weiter!	*Keep on driving!*
das Fahrrad (¨er)	*the bicycle*
der Fahrradweg (e)	*cycle path*
der/die Fahrradfahrer/in (nen)	*cyclist*
die Fahrradroute (n)	*cycle route*
der Fahrradständer (-)	*cycle stand*
die Fahrradversicherung (en)	*cycle insurance*

die Fahrradprüfung (en)   *cycle test*
der Fahrpreis (e)   *ticket price*
die Ermäßigung (en)   *reduction*
die Fahrpreis-
  ermäßigung (en)   *ticket reduction*
das Fahrverbot (e)   *driving ban*

11.2 Travel by train

Core vocabulary

station	der Bahnhof (¨e)
station master	der Bahnhofsbeamte (n)
booking office	der Fahrkartenschalter (-)
timetable	der Zugfahrplan (¨e)
ticket	die Fahrkarte(n)/das Ticket(s)
single ticket	Einfach/Hinfahrkarte
return ticket	Hin und Zurück/
	Rückfahrkarte
arrival	die Ankunft (¨e)
departure	die Abfahrt (en)
indicator board	der Fahrplananzeiger (-)
information	die Information (en)
waiting room	die Wartehalle (n)/der
	Warteraum (¨e)
platform	das Gleis (e)
subway	die Unterführung (en)
stairs	die Treppe (n)
escalator	die Rolltreppe (n)
trains	die Züge
international long-distance	EC (Euro-City)
trains	
high-speed train	ICE (InterCity Express)
fast train	IC (InterCity)
limited-stop fast train	D (Schnellzug)
local train stopping at	RE (Regional Express)
all stations	
limited-stop local train	SE (Städte Express)
suburban services	S-Bahn (Schnellbahn)
underground	U-Bahn
non-smoking	Nichtraucher
smoker	Raucher
first class	Erste Klasse
second class	Zweite Klasse

trolley service	der Essens- und Getränkewagen
restaurant	das Zugrestaurant (s)
personnel	das Zugpersonal (-)
guard	der Schaffner (-)
ticket inspector	der Fahrkartenkontrolleur (e)
train driver	der/die Zugführer/in (-) (en)
traveller	der Passagier (e)
level crossing	der Bahnübergang (¨e)
railway track	die Schiene (-)
signal	das Zugsignal (e)
luggage	das Gepäck
suitcase	der Koffer (-)
left luggage	die Gepäckaufbewahrung

Useful phrases

Do I have to change?	Muss ich umsteigen?
Where do I have to change?	Wo muss ich umsteigen?
Is the train on time?	Fährt der Zug fahrplanmäßig?
How late is the train?	Wie viel Verspätung hat der Zug?
Do we arrive in time?	Kommen wir fahrplanmäßig an?
Which platform does it leave from?	Von welchem Gleis fährt der Zug ab?
Which platform does the train arrive?	Auf welchem Gleis kommt der Zug an?
Is this the train for ...?	Ist das der Zug nach ...?
What time does the train leave?	Um wie viel Uhr fährt der Zug ab?
I have a reservation.	Ich habe einen Platz reserviert.
Sorry, but this is my seat.	Entschuldigen Sie, das ist mein Platz
How often does the train/tram/bus run?	Wie oft fährt der Zug/die Straßenbahn/der Bus?
Which line do I need for ...?	Welche Linie muss ich zum/zur ... nehmen?

Useful verbs

to book a ticket	eine Fahrkarte buchen
to reserve a seat	einen Platz reservieren
to leave luggage	Gepäck <u>auf</u>bewahren

Extras

<u>ein</u>steigen	*to get on*
Alle <u>ein</u>steigen bitte!	*Get on board please!*
<u>um</u>steigen	*to change*
Wo muss ich <u>um</u>steigen?	*Where do I have to change?*
<u>aus</u>steigen	*to get off*
Sie müssen an der nächsten Haltestelle <u>aus</u>steigen.	*You have to get off at the next stop.*
der Zug (¨e)	*the train*
die Verbindung (en)	*the connection*
spät	*late*
die Verspätung (en)	*delay*
sich verspäten	*to be late*
Gibt es eine Verspätung?	*Are we late?*

11.3 Travel by plane

Core vocabulary

airport	der Flughafen (¨)
car park	der Parkplatz (¨e)
departures	der Abflug (¨e)
arrival	die Ankunft (¨e)
booking in	die Flugabfertigung (en)
desk	der Schalter (-)
luggage search	die Gepäckdurchsuchung
security check	die Sicherheitskontrolle (n)
which class?	welche Klasse?
economy	die Touristenklasse/Zweiter Klasse
business	Business Class
first	Erster Klasse
ticket	die Flugkarte (n)/das Ticket (s)
passport	der Reisepass (¨e)

visa	das Visum, das Visa
green card	die Green Card (s)
departure lounge	die Abflughalle(n)
executive lounge	die Executive Lounge
information	der Informationsschalter (-)
announcements	die Ansage (n)
flight	der Flug ("e)
gate	der Flugsteig (e)
delay	die Verspätung (en)
plane	das Flugzeug (e)
row	die Reihe (n)
seat	der Sitz (e)
window seat	der Fensterplatz ("e)
aisle seat	der Gang ("e)
seat belt	der Gurt (e)
life jacket	die Schwimmweste (n)
emergency exit	der Notausgang ("e)
overhead locker	das Handgepäckfach ("er)
toilet	die Toilette (n)
Can I have ...?	Könnte ich bitte ... haben?
earphones	Kopfhörer
a blanket	eine Decke
a pillow	ein Kopfkissen
a drink of water	einen Schluck Wasser
baggage reclaim	die Gepäckrückgabe (n)
baggage processing	die Gepäckabfertigung (en)
customs	der Zoll ("e)
duty-free	zollfrei
emergency landing	die Notlandung (en)
emergency exit	der Notausgang ("e)
pilot	der/die Pilot/in (en) (en)
steward	der Steward (s)
stewardess	die Stewardess (en)
boarding card	die Bordkarte (n)
ticket	der Flugschein (e)

Useful phrases

The plane is delayed.	Das Flugzeug hat Verspätung.
Your flight leaves from gate ...	Ihr Flug fliegt vom Flugsteig ... <u>ab</u>.
Please will you return to your seats and fasten your seat belts.	Bitte kehren Sie zu Ihrem Sitz <u>zurück</u> und schnallen Sie sich <u>an</u>.

We are flying at an altitude of …	Wir fliegen auf einer Höhe von …	181 travel
and a speed of …	und einer Geschwindigkeit von …	
My luggage is missing.	Mein Gepäck ist nicht da.	
I missed my connection flight.	Ich habe meinen Anschlussflug verpasst.	
I can't find my boarding card.	Ich kann meine Bordkarte nicht finden.	

Useful verbs

to leave/depart	<u>ab</u>fliegen
to fly	fliegen
to arrive	<u>an</u>kommen
to land	landen
to navigate	steuern
to put the seat back	den Sitz <u>zurück</u>stellen
to put the seat upright	den Sitz <u>auf</u>stellen
to miss	verpassen
to take off	starten

11.4 Travel by car

Core vocabulary

car	das Auto (s)
estate car	der Kombiwagen (-)
camper	der Campingbus (se)
sports car	das Sportauto (s)
convertible	das Cabrio (s)
automatic	automatisch
2/4 doors	2/4 Türen
pedal	das Pedal (e)
accelerator	das Gaspedal (e)
brake	die Bremse (n)
clutch	die Kupplung (en)
windscreen	die Windschutzscheibe (n)
gears	der Gang (¨e)
gear lever	die Gangschaltung (en)
steering wheel	das Lenkrad (¨er)
handbrake	die Handbremse (n)

indicator	der Blinker (-)
light	das Licht (er)
headlamp	der Scheinwerfer (-)
side light	das Seitenlicht (er)
speedometer	das Geschwindigkeits-messer (-)
milometer	der Kilometerzähler (-)
petrol gauge	die Benzinuhr (en)
interior	die Innenausstattung (en)
seat	der Sitz (e)
safety belt	der Sicherheitsgurt (e)
leg room	der Beinbereich (e)
glove compartment	das Handschuhfach (¨er)
visor/sunshield	die Sonnenblende (n)
wing mirror	der Seitenspiegel (-)
rear mirror	der Rückspiegel (-)
heating	die Heizung (en)
air conditioning	die Klimaanlage (en)
wheel	das Rad (¨er)
tyre	der Reifen (-)
valve	das Ventil (e)
tyre pressure	der Luftdruck
jack	der Wagenheber (-)
spare wheel	der Ersatzreifen (-)
boot	der Kofferraum (¨e)
bonnet	die Motorhaube (n)
bumper	die Stoßstange (n)
number plate	das Nummernschild (er)
foglights	die Nebelleuchte (n)
rear lights	das Rücklicht (er)
exhaust	der Auspuff (e)
battery	die Batterie (n)
radiator	die Heizung (en)
ignition	die Zündung (en)
spark plug	die Zündkerze (n)
water hose	der Wasserschlauch (¨e)
oil pressure	der Öldruck
fan belt	der Gebläseriemen (-)
windscreen wiper	der Scheibenwischer (-)
warning light	das Warnlicht (er)
gear	der Gang (¨e)

Useful phrases

You have left your lights on.	Sie haben/du hast Ihr/dein Licht <u>an</u>gelassen.
How do I move the seat?	Wie kann ich den Sitz verstellen?
How do I open the boot?	Wie öffne ich den Kofferraum?
Does the car have an airbag?	Hat das Auto eine Airbag?

Useful verbs

to exchange	<u>aus</u>wechseln
to put your lights on	das Licht <u>an</u>schalten
to turn your lights off	das Licht <u>aus</u>schalten
to put your indicator on	blinken
to shut	schließen
to check	prüfen
to repair	reparieren

11.5 The road

Core vocabulary

country road	die Landstraße (n)
main road	die Hauptstraße (n)
one-way road	die Einbahnstraße (n)
carriageway	die Fahrbahn (en)
motorway	die Autobahn (en)
motorway lane	die Autospur (en)
inside lane	die Innenbahn (en)
outside lane	die Aussenbahn (en)
access road	die Zugangsstraße (n)
road surface	die Straßenoberfläche (n)
good/bad	gut/schlecht
smooth/uneven	glatt/uneben
bumpy	holprig
potholes	das Schlagloch (¨er)
crossroads	die Kreuzung (en)
dead end	die Sackgasse (n)
roundabout	der Krisverkehr
pedestrian crossing	der Zebrastreifen (-)
bridge	die Brücke (n)

toll bridge	die gebührenpflichtige Brücke (n)
traffic lights	die Ampel (n)
road works	die Straßenarbeiten
emergency traffic lights	das Warnlicht (er)
diversion	die Umleitung (en)
road sign	das Verkehrszeichen (-)
road work	die Bauarbeiten (-)/Baustelle (n)
road narrows	die Fahrbahnverengung (en)
speed limit	die Geschwindigkeits- begrenzung (en)
speed trap	die Radarfalle (n)
traffic police	die Verkehrspolizei
driving licence	der Führerschein (e)
insurance	die Versicherung (en)
fine	die Geldbuße (n)
penalty ticket	der Strafzettel (-)
services	die Dienstleistung (en)
garage	die Werkstatt (¨en)
petrol station	die Tankstelle (n)
petrol	das Benzin
diesel	der Diesel
air	die Luft
water	das Wasser
oil	das Öl
oil change	der Ölwechsel
emergency services	der Notfalldienst (e)
breakdown	die Autopanne (n)

Useful phrases

I have broken down.	Ich habe eine Panne.
The car is overheating.	Das Auto ist überhitzt.
The engine does not start.	Der Motor geht nicht <u>an</u>.
I have a puncture.	Ich habe eine Reifenpanne.
The light does not work.	Das Licht funktioniert nicht.

Useful verbs

to speed	rasen
to accelerate	beschleunigen
to slow down	drosseln
to brake	bremsen
to give way	vorfahrt gewähren
to overtake	<u>über</u>holen

i Typical German road signs

Abstand halten!	*Keep your distance*
Achtung, Achtung!	*Watch! Look out!*
Bauarbeiten	*roadworks*
Durchfahrt verboten	*No through traffic*
Einbahnstraße	*one-way street*
Glatteisgefahr	*icy road*
Keine Einfahrt	*No entry*
Links <u>ab</u>biegen verboten	*No left turn*
Radweg kreuzt	*Cycle path crossing*
Rechts fahren	*Keep right*
Rechts <u>ein</u>biegen	*Turn right*
Sackgasse	*cul-de-sac*
Umleitung	*diversion*
Vorsicht!	*Be careful!*
Vorfahrt beachten	*Give way*

12

tourism

12.1 Where to go

Core vocabulary

tourist industry	die Tourismusindustrie (en)/ die Fremdenverkehrs- industrie (n)
travel agent	das Reisebüro (s)
brochure	der Reiseprospekt (e)
tourist	der Tourist (en)
excursion	der Ausflug (¨e)
tour by bus, car	die Reise (n), die Tour (en), die Fahrt (en)
guided tour by bus	die Rundfahrt(en)
coach trip	die Busfahrt (en)
guided visit	die Führung (en)
cruise	die Kreuzfahrt (en)
adventure holiday	der Abenteuerurlaub (e)
activity holiday	der Aktivitätsurlaub
farm holiday	der Bauernhofurlaub
family holidays	der Familienurlaub
golfing holiday	der Golfurlaub
alternative holidays	die Alternativurlaube
bike holiday	der Fahrradurlaub
sea, sand and sun	Meer, Sand und Sonne
mountains and lakes	Berge und Seen
in the countryside	auf dem Land
to go on holiday	in Urlaub fahren
peak holiday time	die Haupturlaubszeit
national holiday	der Feiertag (e)
tour	die Tour (en)
to go on a tour	auf Tour gehen
to go for a drive/walk/climb	eine Tour machen
long-distance driver	der/die Tourenfahrer/in (¨) (nen)

Useful words and phrases

die Touristen	*tourists*
die Industrie	*industry*
die Touristenindustrie	*tourist industry*
die Touristenklasse	*tourist class*
das Verkehrsamt	*information office*

das Touristenverkehrsamt	*tourist information office*
die Touristenorte	*places for tourists*
die touristischen Attraktionen	*tourist attractions*
der Tourismus	*tourism*

12.2 What to take

Core vocabulary

luggage	das Gepäck
suitcase	der Koffer (-)
travel bag	die Reisetasche (n)
rucksack	der Rucksack (¨e)
hand luggage	das Handgepäck
passport	der Reisepass (¨e)/der Personalausweis (e)
visa	das Visum/das Visa (s)
cash	das Bargeld
insurance	die Versicherung (en)
driving licence	der Führerschein (e)
credit card	die Kreditkarte (n)
currency	die Währung (en)
traveller's cheques	die Reiseschecks
emergency phone number	die Notfallnummer (n)
laptop	der Laptop (s)
mobile phone	das Handy (s)
sponge bag/toilet bag	das Reiseetui (s)
soap	die Seife (n)
toothbrush	die Zahnbürste (n)
toothpaste	die Zahnpasta (s)
razor	der Rasierapparat (e)
nail scissors	die Nagelschere (n)
tweezers	die Pinzette (n)
shampoo	das Shampoo (s)
conditioner	die Pflegespülung
hairbrush	die Haarbürste (n)
comb	der Kamm (¨e)
face creams	die Gesichtscreme
hand cream	die Handcreme (s)
cleanser	der Gesichtsreiniger (-)

moisturizer	die Feuchtigkeitscreme
sun creams	die Sonnencrems
waterproof sun cream	die wasserabweisende Creme (s)
after-sun cream	die Sonnenbrandcreme (s)
factor 10	Faktor 10
wardrobe	der Schrank (¨e)
coat hanger	der Bügel (-)
iron	das Bügeleisen (-)

Useful phrases

I have lost my luggage.	Ich habe mein Gepäck verloren.
I can't find ...	Ich kann ... nicht finden.
Have you got a ...?	Haben Sie ein/e ...?
Where can I get a ...?	Wo kann ich ein/e/en ... bekommen?
Where is the nearest ...?	Wo ist der /die nächste ...?

Useful verbs

to pack	<u>ein</u>packen
to unpack	<u>aus</u>packen
to fold	falten
to hang up	<u>auf</u>hängen
to wash	waschen
to clean	reinigen
to put on	<u>auf</u>tragen
to take along	<u>mit</u>nehmen

12.3 Where to stay

Core vocabulary

accommodation	die Unterkunft (¨e)
two-star hotel	Zwei-Sterne-Hotel
three-star hotel	Drei-Sterne-Hotel
luxury hotel	das Luxushotel
inn	der Gasthof (¨e)
bed and breakfast	die Pension (en), das Gästehaus
holiday house	das Ferienhaus (¨er)

youth hostel	die Jugendherberge (n)
campsite	der Campingplatz (¨e)
caravan site	der Wohnwagenplatz (¨e)
self-catering holiday apartment	die Ferienwohnung (en)
holiday bungalow	der Ferienbungalow (s)
holiday home	das Ferienhaus (¨er)

i Look for signs outside a house or in the window: **Fremdenzimmer frei** or **Zimmer frei**

entrance	der Eingang (¨e)
reception	die Rezeption/der Empfang
night porter	der Nachtportier (s)
manager	der/die Manager/in (-) (nen)
staff	die Angestellten
porter	der Portier (s)
single room	das Einzelzimmer (-)
double room	das Doppelzimmer (-)
twin-bedded room	das Zweibettzimmer (-)
family room	das Familienzimmer (-)
with shower	mit Dusche
with bathroom	mit Bad
with toilet	mit Toilette
with phone	mit Telefon
with television	mit Fernsehen
with internet connection	mit Internetanschluss
with a balcony	mit Balkon
with a sea view	mit Seeblick
with air conditioning	mit Klimaanlage
stairs	die Treppe (n)
lift	der Lift (e), der Aufzug (¨e), der Fahrstuhl (¨e)
restaurant	das Restaurant (s)
fitness room	der Fitnessraum (¨e)
pool	das Schwimmbad (¨er)
hot tub	der Whirlpool
bill	die Rechnung (en)

Useful phrases

Have you got anything ...?	Haben Sie etwas ...?
bigger/smaller	größeres/kleineres
cheaper/better	billigeres/besseres
quieter	ruhigeres
a non-smoking room	ein Nichtraucherzimmer
It is too noisy.	Es ist zu laut.
The shower doesn't work.	Die Dusche geht nicht.
There is no hot water.	Es gibt kein heißes Wasser.
There is no plug in the sink.	Es gibt keinen Stöpsel in dem Waschbecken.

12.4 Camping and caravanning

Core vocabulary

campsite	der Zeltplatz (¨e)
caravan site	der Campingplatz (¨e)
caravan	der Wohnwagen (-)
camper van	das Wohnmobil (e)
trailer	der Anhänger (-)
tent	das Zelt (e)
site	der Platz/die Lage
shady site	die Schattenlage
sunny site	die Sonnenlage
sea view	der Ausblick auf das Meer
mountain view	der Ausblick auf die Berge
facilities	die Einrichtungen
connection	der Anschluss (¨e)
electricity connection	der Elektrizitätsanschluss (¨e)
water connection	der Wasseranschluss (¨e)
running water	fließendes Wasser
drinking water	das Trinkwasser
water tap	der Wasserhahn (¨e)
hook-up	die Schaltung (en)
washrooms	die Waschräume
toilets	die Toiletten
showers	die Duschen
wash basins	die Waschbecken
hairdryers	der Haartrockner/Haarföne
cooking area	die Kochecke

washing-up sinks	die Abwaschbecken
washing machines	die Waschmaschinen
dryers	die Wäschetrockner
drying area	der Trockenraum (¨e)
restaurant	das Restaurant (s)
bar	die Bar (s)
shop	das Geschäft (e)
swimming pool	das Schwimmbad (¨er)
paddling pool	das Planschbecken (-)
children's playground	der Kinderspielplatz (¨e)
swings	die Schaukel (n)
slide	die Rutsche (n)
roundabout	das Karussel (s)
tent	das Zelt (e)
tent pegs	die Zeltpflöcke
guy ropes	das Spannseil (e)
groundsheet	die Unterlegeplane (n)
sleeping bag	der Schlafsack (¨e)
torch	die Taschenlampe (n)
blanket	die Decke (n)
gas cooker	der Gaskocher (-)
gas bottle	die Gasflasche (n)

Useful phrases

Can you help me?	Können Sie mir helfen?
I don't understand how the … works.	Ich verstehe nicht, wie … funktioniert.
Where is the …?	Wo ist der/die/das …?
Is there electricity/water?	Gibt es hier Elektrizität/ Wasser?
Do you have …?	Haben Sie …?
When is the shop open?	Wann ist das Geschäft geöffnet?
Where can I get …?	Wo kann ich … bekommen?

Useful verbs

to tow	ziehen
to park	parken
to put up (tent)	das Zelt <u>auf</u>bauen
to take down (tent)	das Zelt <u>ab</u>bauen
to get wet	nass werden

to wash	waschen
to do the washing	die Wäsche waschen
to dry	trocknen

12.5 What are you going to do?

Core vocabulary

activity holiday	der Aktivitätsurlaub
We want to go ...	Wir wollen ...
swimming	schwimmen gehen
diving	tauchen
water skiing	Wasserski fahren
surfing	surfen
sailing	segeln
walking	spazieren gehen
hiking	wandern
climbing	klettern
gliding	Segelfliegen
paragliding	Paragliding
hanggliding	Drachenfliegen
to play tennis	Tennis spielen
to play volleyball	Volleyball spielen
to go bike riding	Fahrrad fahren gehen
sights	die Sehenswürdigkeiten
monuments	die Monumente, die Denkmäler
castles	die Schlösser/Burgen
archeological sites	die archäologischen Stätten
ancient monuments	uralte Monumente
historic buildings	geschichtliche Gebäude
scenery	die Landschaft
animals	die Tiere

Useful phrases

What is there to see/do?	Was gibt es dort ... zu sehen/tun?
Is it suitable for ...?	Ist es für ... geeignet?
older people	ältere Leute
younger people	jüngere Leute
children	Kinder

Useful verbs

to *have a good time*	sich vergnügen
to *have a rest*	sich <u>aus</u>ruhen
to *relax*	sich entspannen
to *do nothing*	nichts tun
to *laze about*	faulenzen/gammeln
to *go skiing*	Skifahren
to *go snowboarding*	Snowboard fahren
to *go sledging*	Schlitten fahren/rodeln
to *go ice skating*	Schlittschuh laufen
to *sun oneself*	sich sonnen

12.6 On the beach

Core vocabulary

sea	das Meer/die See
coast	die Küste (n)
beach	der Strand (¨e)
bay	die Bucht (en)
shore	das Ufer (-)
sand	der Sand
rocks	die Felsen
high tide	die Flut (-)
low tide	die Ebbe (-)
waves	die Wellen
beach bar	die Strandbar (s)
windbreak	der Windschutz
shelter	der Schutz
parasol	der Sonnenschirm (e)
lounger	die Sonneliege (n)
deckchair	der Liegestuhl (¨e)
air mattress	die Luftmatratze (n)
shower	die Dusche (n)
towel	das Handtuch (¨er)
swimming costume	der Schwimmanzug (¨e)
trunks	die Badhose (n)
bikini	der Bikini (s)
sun lotion	die Sonnencreme (s)
sun glasses	die Sonnenbrille (n)
rubber ring	der Gummiring (e)
swimming cap	die Bademütze (n)

sandcastle	die Sandburg (en)
bucket	der Eimer (-)
spade	der Spaten (-)
kite	der Drachen (-)
snorkel	der Schnorchel (-)
flippers	die Schwimmflossen
inflatable	aufblasbar
pump	pumpen
surfboard	das Surfbrett (er)
wind surfer	der Windsurfer (-)
waterski	der Wasserski (er)
fishes	die Fische
shells	die Muscheln
octopus	die Kraken
squid	die Tintenfische
mussels	die Muscheln
scallops	die Jakobsmuscheln
shrimps	die Garnelen
jellyfish	die Qualle (n)

Useful phrases

The tide is in.	Es ist Flut.
The tide is out.	Es ist Ebbe.
It is safe for bathing/swimming.	Es ist sicher zu baden/ schwimmen.
I have been stung by a jellyfish.	Ich bin von einer Qualle gestochen worden.
The water is too deep.	Das Wasser ist zu tief.
He/she can't swim.	Er/sie kann nicht schwimmen.
He/she needs help.	Er/sie braucht Hilfe.
Help!	Hilfe!
Attention!	Achtung!

Useful verbs

to snorkel	schnorcheln
to sunbathe	sonnenbaden
to relax	entspannen/relaxen
to play	spielen
to dig	buddeln
to dive	tauchen

to sting	stechen
to splash around	planschen

12.7 At sea

Core vocabulary

canoe	das Kanu (s)
motor boat	das Motorboot (e)
rubber dinghy	das Schlauchboot (e)
rowing boat	das Ruderboot (e)
sailing boat	das Segelboot (e)
sailing ship	das Segelschiff (e)
surfboard	das Surfbrett (er)
waterski	der Wasserski (er)
wind surfer	der/die Windsurfer/in (-) (nen)
yacht	die Yacht (en)
MAYDAY	MAYDAY
SOS	SOS
lifeboat	das Rettungsboot (e)
lifejacket	die Lebensrettungsjacke (n)
lifeguard	der/die Bademeister/in (-) (nen) Strandmeister/in (-) (nen)
flare	die Leuchtkugel (n)/das Leuchtsignal (e)
weather forecast	die Wettervorhersage (n)
the sea is ...	die See ist ...
calm	ruhig
rough	rauh
windforce	die Windstärke
galeforce	die Orkanstärke
rain	der Regen
visibility	die Sicht
foggy	neblig
equipment	die Ausrüstung (en)
compass	der Kompass (e)
sail	das Segel (-)
hull	der Rumpf
cabin	die Kabine (n)
berth	die Koje (n)
wheel	das Steuerrad (¨er)
starboard	das Steuerbord
harbour, port	der Hafen (¨)

lighthouse	der Leuchtturm (¨ e)
the coast	die Küste (n)
cliffy coast	die Kliffküste (n)
the coastguard	die Küstenwache
sea coast	die Seeküste (n)
west coast	die Westküste

Useful verbs

to moor	<u>fest</u>machen
to chain	<u>an</u>ketten
to anchor	Anker legen
to sail	segeln
to navigate	navigieren
to steer	steuern
to tie up/moor	<u>fest</u>binden
to anchor	verankern
to rescue	retten
to be rescued	gerettet sein

12.8 The great outdoors

Core vocabulary

rucksack	der Rucksack (¨ e)
sleeping bag	der Schlafsack (¨ e)
ground mat/mattress	die Bodenmatratze (n)
torch	die Taschenlampe (n)
penknife	das Taschenmesser (-)
compass	der Kompass (e)
map	die Karte (n)
water bottle	die Wasserflasche (n)
camping stove	der Campingkocher (-)
matches	die Streichhölzer
lighter	das Feuerzeug (e)
gas container	die Gasflasche (n)
billy can	der Wasserkessel (-)
bowl	die Schüssel (n)
knife	das Messer
fork	die Gabel
spoon	der Löffel (n)
plate	der Teller (-)
mug	der Becher (-)
emergency rations	die Notfallrationen

dried food	getrocknetes Essen
dried fruit	das Trockenobst
nuts	die Nüsse
chocolate	die Schokolade
transceiver (for snow rescue)	das Verschüttungsgerät
mobile phone	das Handy (s)
batteries	die Batterien
charger	das Aufladegerät (e)
plug	der Stecker (-)
waterproofs	wasserdichte Kleidung
spare clothing	Kleidung zum Umziehen
rope	das Seil (e)
climbing harness	der Klettergurt (e)
climbing gear	die Kletterausrüstung (en)
crampons	das Steigeisen (-)
boots	die Stiefel (-)
ice axe	der Eispickel (-)

Useful phrases

My feet are sore.	Meine Füße tun weh.
My back is sore.	Mein Rücken tut weh.
I need extra socks.	Ich brauche extra Socken.
I have blisters.	Ich habe Blasen.
Do you have plasters?	Haben Sie Pflaster?
antiseptic cream	antiseptische Creme
insect repellent	Insektenschutzmittel
antihistamine cream (for insect bites)	das Antihistaminikum
Have you got something for …?	Haben Sie etwas gegen …?
I have been stung by a wasp/ bee/mosquito.	Ich bin von einer Wespe/ Biene/Mücke gestochen worden.
I have been bitten by …	Ich bin von … gebissen worden.
by a snake	von einer Schlange
by a dog	von einem Hund

13 the body and health

13.1 The face

Core vocabulary

head	der Kopf (¨e)
face	das Gesicht (er)
hair	das Haar (e)
forehead	die Stirn (en)
ears	die Ohren
eyes	die Augen
eyebrows	die Augenbrauen
eyelashes	die Augenwimpern
nose	die Nase (n)
nostrils	der Nasenflügel (-)
cheeks	die Wangen
chin	das Kinn (e)
mouth	der Mund (¨er)
lips	die Lippen
tongue	die Zunge (n)
tooth	der Zahn (¨e)
neck	der Hals (¨e)

Useful phrases

He has	Er hat
a beard	einen Bart
moustache	einen Schnurrbart
He/she wears glasses.	Er/sie trägt eine Brille.
contact lenses	Kontaktlinsen
I am short sighted/	Ich bin kurzsichtig/
long sighted.	langsichtig.

i Remember **die Brille** is singular in German.
Die runde Brille *ist* **schön.**
The round glasses *are* nice.

Useful verbs

to hear	hören
to see	sehen
to smell	riechen
to taste	schmecken

to *feel*	fühlen
to *sleep*	schlafen
to *smile*	lächeln
to *laugh*	lachen
to *talk*	sprechen
to *shout*	schimpfen
to *cry*	weinen
to *snore*	schnarchen
to *hiccup*	<u>auf</u>stoßen
to *cough*	husten
to *touch*	berühren

Extras

I have ... a headache	Ich habe ... Kopfschmerzen
toothache	Zahnschmerzen
earache	Ohrenschmerzen
a nose bleed	Nasenbluten
My eyes are sore.	Meine Augen tun weh.
to have a facial	eine Gesichtsbehandlung haben
to have your hair done	das Haar gemacht bekommen
to have a nose job	eine Nasenoperation haben
to have plastic surgery	eine Schönheitsoperation haben
to have wrinkles	Falten haben
to have a nice smile	ein nettes Lächeln haben
shampoo	das Haarwaschmittel (-)/ Shampoo (s)
conditioner	das Haarpflegemittel (-)
face cream	die Gesichtscreme (s)
moisturizer	die Feuchtigkeitscreme (s)
face pack	die Gesichtspackung (en)
lip salve	die Lippencreme (s)
shaving cream	der Rasierschaum
shaving brush	der Rasierpinsel (-)
razor	die Rasierklinge (n)
after-shave lotion	die Aftershave-Lotion/ das Rasierwasser
make-up	das Make-up
mascara	die Wimperntusche (n)
lipstick	der Lippenstift (e)
eye shadow	der Lidschatten (-)
powder	das Puder (-)

13.2 The body

Core vocabulary

shoulder	die Schulter (n)
arm	der Arm (e)
elbow	der Ellenbogen
wrist	das Armgelenk (e)
hand	die Hand (¨e)
finger	der Finger
thumb	der Daumen (-)
fingernail	die Fingernagel (¨)
body	der Körper
chest	die Brust
breasts	der Busen
nipple	die Brustwarze (n)
waist	die Taille (n)
hips	die Hüfte (n)
abdomen	der Unterleib (e)
bottom	der Hintern (-) /der Po (s)
sexual organs	die Sexualorgane
penis	der Penis
testicles	die Hoden
vagina	die Vagina/die Scheide
leg	das Bein (e)
thigh	der Oberschenkel (-)
knee	das Knie (e)
ankle	der Fußknöchel
foot	der Fuß (¨e)
toe	der Zeh (en)
heel	die Fersen/die Hacke (n)
back	der Rücken
front	die Vorderseite (n)
side	die Seite (n)
internal organs	die inneren Organe
brain	das Gehirn
stomach	der Magen (¨)
throat	der Hals (¨e)
lung	die Lunge (n)
kidney	die Niere (n)
heart	das Herz (en)
blood	das Blut
veins	die Vene (n)
arteries	die Arterie (n)
blood transfusion	die Bluttransfusion (en)

blood donor	die Blutspende
blood type	die Blutgruppe
intestines	die Innereien
skeleton	das Skelett (e)
bone	der Knochen (-)
joint	das Gelenk (e)
nervous system	das Nervensystem (e)
nerve	der Nerv (en)
circulation	die Zirkulation (en)
breathing	die Atmung
digestion	die Verdauung

Useful phrases

I have ...	Ich habe ...
stomachache	Magenschmerzen
heart burn	Sodbrennen
indigestion	Magenverstimmung
high/low blood pressure	hohen/niedrigen Blutdruck
My feet/hands/legs hurt.	Meine Füße/Hände/Beine tun weh.

Useful verbs

to feel	fühlen
to touch	berühren
to stroke	streicheln
to massage	massieren
to hold	halten
to embrace	umarmen
to kiss	küssen
to kick	treten
to walk	gehen
to run	rennen
to jump	springen

13.3 I need a doctor

Core vocabulary

doctor	der Arzt (¨e), die Ärztin (nen)
eye specialist	Augen**arzt**
paediatrician	Kinder**arzt**
ear, nose and throat specialist	Halsnasenohren**arzt**
internist	Fach**arzt** für Innere Medizin (Internist)
general practitioner (GP)	Fach**arzt** für Allgemeinmedizin
gynaecologist	der/die Gynäkologe/Frauen**arzt**
general practitioner	praktischer **Arzt**
orthopaedic specialist	**Arzt** für Orthopädie
heart specialist	der/die Herzspezialist/in
dentist	Zahn**arzt**
appointment	der Termin (e)
surgery	die Arztpraxis (praxen)

Useful phrases

I have a pain …	Ich habe Schmerzen …
It hurts.	Es tut weh.
I don't feel well.	Mir geht es nicht gut.
I can't sleep/eat/walk …	Ich kann nicht schlafen, essen/gehen.
I am pregnant.	Ich bin schwanger.
I am in the menopause.	Ich bin in den Wechseljahren.
I feel sick.	Mir ist schlecht.
I feel dizzy.	Mir ist schwindlig.
I have got spots.	Ich habe Pickel.
I have been bitten/stung.	Ich bin gebissen/gestochen worden.

Ailments

cold	die Erkältung (en)
flu (influenza)	die Grippe (n)
measles	Masern
mumps	Mumps
German measles	Röteln
tonsillitis	die Mandelentzündung (en)
cough	der Husten

sore throat	das Halsweh
indigestion	die Magenverstimmung (en)
hypertension	der Hypertonie/der erhöhte Blutdruck
constipation	die Verstopfung
diarrhoea	der Durchfall
AIDS	das Aids
HIV	das HIV
polio	die Kinderlähmung
hepatitis	die Hepatitis
rabies	die Tollwut
typhoid	der Typhus
typhus	das Fleckfieber
cholera	die Cholera
yellow fever	das Gelbfieber
malaria	die Malaria
cancer	der Krebs
multiple sclerosis	die multiple Sklerose (MS)

Useful words and phrases

I am allergic to ...	Ich bin allergisch gegen ...
penicillin	Penizillin
nuts	Nüsse
animals	Tiere
I have hay fever.	Ich habe Heuschnupfen.
asthma	Asthma
He needs an inhaler.	Er braucht ein Inhalations- gerät.
She is handicapped.	Sie ist behindert.
She is paraplegic.	Sie ist gelähmt.
She has her period.	Sie hat ihre Periode.
He is in puberty.	Er ist in der Pubertät.
an injection/a jab for	eine Injektion/Spritze gegen
immunization	die Immunisierung
inoculation	die Impfung (en)
health certificate	der Gesundheitspass
examination	die Untersuchung
x-ray	die Röntgenaufnahme
I have broken my leg/ankle/ wrist.	Ich habe mein Bein/mein Fußgelenk/mein Handgelenk gebrochen.

plaster	das Pflaster (-)
crutches	die Krücken
walking stick	der Krückstock (¨e)
wheel chair	der Rollstuhl (¨e)

Useful verbs

to go to bed	zu Bett gehen
to sleep	schlafen
to take more exercise	sich mehr bewegen
to eat less	weniger essen
to avoid	vemeiden

Extras

medicine	die Medizin
conventional medicine	die Schulmedizin
alternative medicine	die alternative Medizin
pills	die Pillen
pain killers	Schmerztabletten
vitamin supplements	Vitamintabletten
injection	die Spritze (n)
cure	die Heilung
homeopathic remedy	homöopathische Mittel
physiotherapy	die Physiotherapie
aromatherapy	die Aromatherapie
reflexology	die Reflexologie
sleep	der Schlaf
rest	<u>aus</u>ruhen
to recover	sich erholen

13.4 At the hospital

Core vocabulary

hospital	das Krankenhaus (¨er)
department	die Abteilung (en)
emergency	der Notfall (¨e)
doctor	der/die Arzt/¨in (¨e) (nen)
nurse	der/die Krankenpfleger/in (-) (nen)
ward	die Station (en)

bed	das Bett (en)
anaesthetic	die Anästhesie (n)/die Narkose (n)
surgery	die Chirurgie
operation	die Operation (en)
operating theatre	der Operationssaal (¨e)

Health resorts

die Kur (en)	spa
der Kurort (e)	health resort
das Kurhaus (¨er)	assembly rooms at health resort
der Kurgast (¨e)	visitor to a spa
der Kurpark (s)	spa park
das Kurwasser	spa water
das Kurkonzert (e)	spa concert
kuren	to take a cure, take the spa water
das Thermalbad (¨er)	thermal bath
der Fango	mud bath
die Massage (n)	massage

i The emergency doctor service is called **Ärztlicher Notfalldienst**:

a house call	Ärztlicher Hausbesuch
dental emergencies	Zahnärztlicher Notfalldienst
chemist	die Apotheke (n)
chemist	die Drogerie (n)

i There are two types of chemist: **Apotheke** and **Drogerie**. To get a prescription from your doctor you have to go to the **Apotheke**.

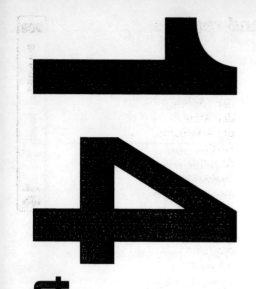

14

the world

14.1 Geography and regions

Core vocabulary

world	die Welt
earth	die Erde
globe	der Globus
atlas	der Atlas
continents	die Kontinente
Africa	Afrika
America	Amerika
North America	Nordamerika
South America	Südamerika
Asia	Asien
Australia	Australien
Europe	Europa
the Arctic	die Arktis
the Antarctic	die Antarktis
the Middle East	der Nahe Osten
the Far East	der Ferne Osten
India	Indien
China	China
Japan	Japan
Indonesia	Indonesien
New Zealand	Neuseeland
Pacific Islands	die Pazifischen Inseln

14.2 The countries of Europe

Austria	Österreich
Belgium	Belgien
Denmark	Dänemark
Finland	Finnland
France	Frankreich
Germany	Deutschland
Greece	Griechenland
Ireland	Irland
Italy	Italien
Luxembourg	Luxemburg
Netherlands	die Niederlande
Portugal	Portugal
Spain	Spanien

Sweden	Schweden
United Kingdom	Großbritannien
Norway	Norwegen
Iceland	Island
Switzerland	die Schweiz
Turkey	die Türkei
Russia	Russland
Lithuania	Litauen
Latvia	Lettland
Estonia	Estland
Bulgaria	Bulgarien
Romania	Rumänien
Bosnia	Bosnien
Slovenia	Slovenien
Croatia	Kroatien
Poland	Polen
Hungary	Ungarn
Czech Republic	die Tschechische Republik
England	England
Scotland	Schottland
Northern Ireland	Nordirland
Wales	Wales
Ireland	Irland
European Union	die Europäische Union
European Parliament	das Europäische Parlament
Common Market	der gemeinsamer Markt
member of the European parliament	Mitglieder des Europäischen Parlaments
common agricultural policy	die gemeinsame Landwirtschaftspolitik
euro	der Euro
European institutions	die Europäischen Institutionen
European bank	die Europäische Bank

14.3 The high seas!

Core vocabulary

points of the compass	die Kompassrichtungen
north	der Norden
south	der Süden
east	der Osten

west	der Westen
northeast	der Nordosten
southwest	der Südwesten
ocean	der Ozean (e)
Atlantic	der Atlantische Ozean
Indian	der Indische Ozean
Pacific	der Pazifische Ozean
Arctic	das Nordpolarmeer
Antarctic	das Südpolarmeer
Mediterranean	das Mittelmeer
North Sea	die Nordsee
Baltic	die Ostsee
Red Sea	das Rote Meer
English Channel	der Ärmelkanal
navigation	die Navigation
longitude	das Längengrad
latitude	das Breitengrad
equator	der Äquator
northern hemisphere	die Nordhalbkugel
southern hemisphere	die Südhalbkugel
tropics	die Tropen
bay	die Bucht (en)
island	die Insel (n)
peninsula	die Halbinsel (n)
canal	der Kanal (¨e)
Suez Canal	der Sueskanal
Panama Canal	der Panamakanal
straits	die Meerenge (n)
currents	die Strömungen
tides	die Gezeiten
ferry	die Fähre (n)
liner	das Passagierschiff (e)
cruise ship	das Kreuzfahrtschiff (e)
tanker	der Tanker (-)
container ship	das Containerschiff (e)
hazards	Gefahren
icebergs	der Eisberg (e)
shipping	die Schifffahrt
shipping line	die Schifffahrtslinie
storm, gale	der Sturm (¨e)
galeforce	die Sturmstärke
rough seas	rauhe See
calm seas	ruhige See

Useful verbs

to board	besteigen
to embark	<u>ein</u>schiffen
to disembark	<u>aus</u>schiffen
to disembark	von Bord gehen

14.4 The weather forecast

Core vocabulary

weather report	der Wetterbericht (e)
rain	der Regen
snow	der Schnee
wind	der Wind
fog	der Nebel
sun	die Sonne
hail	der Hagel
sleet	der Schneeregen
thunder	der Donner (-)
lightning	der Blitz (e)
it is raining	es regnet
it is rainy	es ist regnerisch
the rainy season	die Regenzeit
shower of rain	der Regenschauer (-)
light rain	leichter Regen
umbrella	der Regenschirm (e)
rainwear	die Regenkleidung
sunbeam	der Sonnenstrahl (en)
sunrise	der Sonnenaufgang (¨e)
sunset	der Sonnenuntergang (¨e)
solar eclipse	die Sonnenfinsternis
position of the sun	der Sonnenstand
the sun is shining	die Sonne scheint
it is sunny	es ist sonnig
the heat	die Hitze
heat stroke	der Hitzschlag (¨e)
heatwave	die Hitzewelle (n)

Useful phrase

Mein Mann ist hitzeempfindlich. *My husband is sensitive to heat.*

Degrees of temperature

warmth	die Wärme
it is warm	es ist warm
cold	die Kälte
cold weather front	die Kaltwetterfront
cold spell	der Kälteeinbruch
5 degrees	5 Grad
it is cold	es ist kalt
it is freezing	es ist eiskalt

Useful words and phrases

I shiver with cold.	Ich zittere vor Kälte.
The cold is getting to me.	Die Kälte macht mir zu schaffen.
it is snowing	es schneit
snowstorm	der Schneesturm (¨e)
frost	der Frost
it is frosty	es ist frostig
cloud	die Wolke (-)
it is cloudy	es ist bewölkt
clear sky	wolkenlos
sky	der Himmel (-)
dryness	die Trockenheit
dry	trocken
wetness	die Feuchtigkeit
it is wet	es ist feucht
humidity	die Luftfeuchtigkeit
humid	feucht
dampness	die Nässe
it is damp	es ist nass
The constant wetness is getting to my bones.	Die ewige Nässe fährt mir in die Knochen.
today	heute
tomorrow	morgen
over the next few days	für die nächsten Tage
the weather is getting worse	das Wetter wird schlimmer
is improving	das Wetter verbessert sich
stays the same	das Wetter bleibt so
dangerous driving conditions	gefährliche Fahrbedingungen
risk of flooding	Überflutungsgefahr
danger of black ice	Glatteisgefahr

the temperature is ...	die Temperatur beträgt ...
degrees	das Grad
Centigrade	das Grad Celsius
Fahrenheit	das Grad Fahrenheit
the temperature is rising/falling	die Temperatur steigt/fällt
maximum temperature	die Höchsttemperatur
minimum temperature	die Mindesttemperatur
cloudy	bedeckt
light rain at times	zeitweise leichter Regen
becoming less cloudy	zurückgehende Bewölkung
light	schwach
lowest temperature	die Tiefstwerte

15
government and society

15.1 Politics and government

Core vocabulary

politics	die Politik
government	die Regierung (en)
democracy	die Demokratie (en)
dictatorship	die Diktatur (en)
monarchy	die Monarchie (n)
federal president	der Bundespräsident (en)
prime minister	der Premierminister (-)
member of parliament	der/die Abgeordnete (n)
head of state	das Staatsoberhaupt (¨er)
party leader	der/die Partievorsitzende (n)
members of parliament	die Parlamentsmitglieder
constituency	die Konstitution (en)
election	die Wahl (en)
vote	die Stimme (n)
parliament	das Parlament (e)
foreign minister	der Außenminister (-)
home secretary	der Innenminister (-)
minister of defence	der Verteidigungsminister (-)
minister of agriculture	der Landwirtschaftsminister (-)
finance minister	der Finanzminister (-)
local government	die Kommunalverwaltung (en)
town hall	das Rathaus (¨er)
town council	der Stadtrat (¨e)
town councillors	die Stadträte
local taxes	die Gemeindesteuer (n)
job centre	das Arbeitsamt (¨er)
social services	die Sozialeinrichtungen
social welfare office	das Sozialamt (¨er)

Useful verbs

to make a speech	eine Ansprache halten
to debate	debattieren
to vote	wählen
to pass a bill	ein Gesetz verabschieden
to pay taxes	Steuern bezahlen

More vocabulary

army	die Armee/das Militär
German Army	die Bundeswehr

soldier	der/die Soldat/in (en) (nen)
to invade	<u>ein</u>marschieren
navy	die Marine
sailor	der Matrose (n)
to sail	segeln
warship	das Kriegsschiff (e)
airforce	die Luftwaffe
pilot	der/die Pilot/in (en)
jet fighter	Düsenjäger (-)
to fly	fliegen
peacekeeping force	die Friedenstruppe (n)
to withdraw troops	Truppen <u>ab</u>ziehen
to agree on something	etwas vereinbaren
to avoid war	den Krieg vermeiden
police force	die Polizei
policeman	der/die Polizist/in (en) (nen)
police car	das Polizeiauto (s)
to arrest	verhaften

Useful phrases

the war against terrorism	der Kampf gegen den Terrorismus
to carry out an attack	einen Anschlag verüben
terrorist attack	der terroristiche Anschlag
bomb attack	der Bombenanschlag
to hijack a plane	ein Flugzeug entführen
to take a hostage	Geiseln nehmen
suicide bomber	Selbstmordattentäter

Useful verbs

to defend	verteidigen
to fight	kämpfen
to guard/protect	beschützen
to spy	spionieren
to attack	<u>an</u>greifen
to occupy	besetzen
to wound	verletzen

Vocabulary for peace

peace	der Frieden
to make one's peace	Frieden schließen

movement	die Bewegung (en)
peace movement	die Friedensbewegung (en)
negotiation	die Verhandlung (en)
peace negotiations	die Friedensverhandlungen (en)
conference	die Konferenz (e)
peace conference	die Friedenskonferenz
Nobel Peace Prize	der Friedensnobelpreis
to be peaceful	friedlich sein
peace loving	friedliebend

15.2 Local government and services

Core vocabulary

police	die Polizei
emergency services	Notfalldienste
ambulance	der Krankenwagen (-)
fire brigade	die Feuerwehr (en)
telephone	das Telefon (e)
electricity	die Elektrizität
gas	das Gas
water	das Wasser
mayor	der Bürgermeister (-)
town hall	das Rathaus ("er)
local council	die Kommunalverwaltung (en)
roads	die Straßen
transport	der Verkehr
tourist office	das Touristeninformations-büro
council offices	die Stadtverwaltung (en)
taxes	die Steuern
council tax	die Gemeindesteuer (n)
bureaucracy	die Bürokratie (n)
small print	das Kleingedruckte
civil servant	der Beamte (n)/ die Beamtin (nen)
paperwork	die Papierarbeit
pass	der Pass ("e)
permit	die Genehmigung (en)
resident's permit	der Aufenthaltsgenehmigung (en)
receipt	der Beleg (e)
driving licence	der Führerschein (e)
insurance	die Versicherung (en)
medical insurance	die Krankenversicherung (en)

medical check	die ärztliche (n) Untersuchung (en)
solicitor	der/die Rechtsanwalt/¨in (¨e) (nen)
criminal lawyer	der/die Anwalt/in (¨e) (nen)
criminal offence	die Straftat (en)
court	das Gericht (e)
sentence	das Urteil (e)
fine	die Buße (n)
imprisonment	die Inhaftierung (en)
local taxes	die Gemeindesteuern

Useful phrases

I don't understand that.	Ich verstehe das nicht.
I don't understand you.	Ich verstehe Sie nicht.
I didn't know.	Ich wusste das nicht.
I have already supplied you with this document.	Ich habe Ihnen das Dokument schon gegeben.
I need help.	Ich brauche Hilfe.
Is there anyone who can help me?	Gibt es jemanden, der mir helfen kann?
When are the offices open?	Wann ist das Büro geöffnet?
Where do I need to go to get ...?	Wohin muss ich gehen, um ... zu bekommen?
What do I need?	Was brauche ich?
Where can I get it?	Wo kann ich es bekommen?

15.3 Money

Core vocabulary

currency	die Währung (en)
dollars	die Dollars
sterling	das Pfund
euro	der Euro (s)
cent	der Cent (s)
cash	das Bargeld
eurocheques	die Euroschecks
bank	die Bank (en)
bank account	das Bankkonto (konten)
current account	das Girokonto (konten)

savings account	das Sparkonto (konten)
deposit	die Anzahlung (en)
account number	die Kontonummer (n)
bank sort code	die Bankleitzahl (en)
cheque book	das Scheckbuch (¨er)
credit card	die Kreditkarte (n)
cheque card	die Scheckkarte (n)
signature	die Unterschrift (en)
PIN number	die Geheimnummer (n)
loan	das Darlehen (-)
overdraft	der Überziehungskredit (e)
bank transfer	die Banküberweisung (en)
in credit	im Haben
in the red	im Soll
bankruptcy	der Bankrott
mortgage	die Hypothek (en)
household insurance	die Hausratversicherung (en)
stocks and shares	Börse und Aktien
stock market	der Börsenmarkt (¨e)
prices	die Preise
dividend	die Dividende (n)
profits	der Profit (e)
loss	der Verlust (e)
inflation	die Inflation

Useful verbs

to apply	beantragen
to be accepted	angenommen sein
to be refused	verweigert sein
to win	gewinnen
to lose	verlieren
to make a gain	einen Gewinn machen
to make a loss	einen Verlust machen
to buy/sell shares	Aktien kaufen/verkaufen
to save	sparen

Allowances and taxes

accounts	die Buchhaltung
accountant	der Buchhalter/in (-) (nen)/ Steuerberater/in (-) (nen)
annual accounts	jährliche Buchführung

income tax	die Lohnsteuer/
	Einkommenssteuer
tax class	die Steuerklasse
church tax	die Kirchensteuer
child allowance	der Kinderfreibetrag
employee expenses	der Arbeitnehmer-Pauschalbetrag
threshold level	der Grundfreibetrag
income tax table	die Einkommensteuertabelle
inheritance tax	die Erbschaftssteuer

15.4 National holidays

Public and state holidays

i Public holidays
24 December *Christmas Eve* **Weihnachtsabend**
25 December **1. Weihnachtstag**
26 December **2. Weihnachtstag**
31 December *New Year's Eve* **Sylvester**
1 January *New Year's Day* **Neujahr**
March or April *Good Friday* **Karfreitag**
Easter Monday **Ostermontag**
1 May *May Day* or *Labour Day* **1. Mai** oder **Tag der Arbeit**
3 October *Day of Unification* **Tag der Deutschen Einheit**

i Individual **Land** holidays
6 January *Epiphany* **Heilige Drei Könige**
May or June   *Ascension Day* **Himmelfahrtstag**
                  Pentecost or *Whitsun* **Pfingsten, Pfingstmontag**
                  Corpus Christi **Fronleichnam**
1 November *All Saints Day* **Allerheiligen**

Germany is known for its **Karneval** (*carnival*) which is celebrated in cities like Mainz, Cologne and Bonn but recently Berlin started to have some **Karnevalsumzüge** on **Rosenmontag** (*Rose Monday Parade*) as well.

The *crazy days* **Verrückten Tage** are on **Rosenmontag**, the 42nd day before Easter.

Core vocabulary

| village fete | das Dorffest |
| circus | der Zirkus |

concert	das Konzert (e)
band	die Band (s)
gig	der Gig (s)
competition	der Wettbewerb (e)
music competition	der Musikwettbewerb (e)

ℹ Other festivals

the Love Parade
Potsdam Bachtage
Chiemsee Reggae Summer Festival
Dresden Music Festival
Salzburger Festspiele
Potsdamer Jazz Festival
Wagner Festpiele
Handel Festspiele Halle

Munich has its famous **Oktoberfest**, which begins in September.
Wine festivals (**Weinfeste**) take place along the Rhine and Moselle
rivers.

ℹ *National dress* (**die Trachtenkleidung**)

das Dirndl ⎫
die Lederhose ⎬ in Bavaria
der Schwarzwaldhut (Bollenhut) in the Black Forest

15.5 Environmental issues

Core vocabulary

environment	die Umwelt
environmentalist	der/die Umweltschützer/in (-) (nen)
environmental issues	die Umweltfragen
environmental health	die Umweltbelastung (en)
public health	das Gesundheitswesen
housing	das Wohnungswesen
architect	der/die Architekt/in (en) (nen)
builder	der Bauherr (en)/Baumeister (-)
planner	der/die Stadtplaner/in (-) (nen)
planning permission	die Baugenehmigung (en)
building regulations	die Bauauflage (n)
water	das Wasser
electricity	die Elektrizität
sewage	das Abwasser
water level	der Wasserstand

drinking water	das Trinkwasser
water supply	die Wasserversorgung
well	der Brunnen (-)
irrigation	die Bewässerung
ecology	die Ökologie
ecosystem	das Ökosystem (e)
erosion	die Erosion (en)
GM	manipulierte Nahrungsmittel
organic	organisch
artificial fertilizer	der künstliche Dünger
nitrates	dic Nitrate
pesticides	die Pestizide
poison	das Gift
weedkiller	die Unkrautvernichter (-)
pollution	die Verschmutzung
environmental pollution	die Umweltverschmutzung
acid rain	saurer Regen
air pollution	die Luftverschmutzung
car exhaust	die Autoabgase
detergent	die Reinigungsmittel
biodegradable detergent	biologisch abbaubare Reinigungsmittel
global warming	die Erwärmung der Erdatmosphäre
greenhouse gas	das Treibhausgas
nuclear testing	nukleare Tests
hole in the ozone layer	das Ozonloch
radiation	die radioaktive Strahlung
radioactive waste	der radioaktive Abfall
water pollution	die Wasserverschmutzung
energy	die Energie
nuclear power	die Atomenergie
electric power	die elektrische Energie
solar power	die Solarenergie/ Sonnenenergie
wind power	die Windenergie
power station	das Kraftwerk/das Elektrizitätswerk
national park	der Nationalpark (s)
regions of special scientific interest	Gebiete von besonderem wissenschaftlichem Interesse
protected area	geschützte Gegenden
conservation area	das Landschaftsschutzgebiet (e)
listed building	denkmalgeschütztes Gebäude

ancient monument	die Denkmalpflege
archaeological site	das archäologische Gebiet

Recycling

der Müll	*rubbish*
das Glas	*glass*
die Flasche (n)	*bottle*
weiß	*white/clear*
grün	*green*
braun	*brown*
weißes Papier	*white paper*
das Buntpapier	*coloured paper*
der Plastikmüll	*plastic articles*
die Plastiktüten	*plastic bags*
die Leinentaschen	*linen bags*
der Restmüll	*non-organic waste*
der Biomüll	*organic waste*
die Papierabfuhr	*paper collection*
die gelben Säcke	*yellow bags*

Greenpeace

protection of the environment	der Umweltschutz
of animals	der Tierschutz
of plants	der Pflanzenschutz
of oceans	der Schutz der Ozeane
of forests	der Schutz der Wälder

Useful phrases

to draw attention to	die Aufmerksamkeit lenken auf
global environmental problems	globale Umweltprobleme
threat to the natural environment	die Bedrohung der natürlichen Umwelt

Useful verbs

to protect	beschützen
to conserve	erhalten, schonen
to destroy	zerstören
to dispose of	beseitigen
to throw away	wegwerfen

15.6 Religion

Core vocabulary

religion	die Religion (en)
belief	der Glaube (n)
Buddhism	der Buddhismus
Christianity	das Christentum
Hinduism	der Hinduismus
Islam	der Islam
Judaism	das Judentum
agnostic	agnostisch
atheist	der/die Atheist/in (en) (nen)
Buddhist	der/die Buddhist/in (en) (nen)
Catholic	der/die Katholik/in (en) (nen)
Christian	der/die Christ/in (en) (nen)
Hindu	der/die Hinduist/in (en) (nen)
Jew	der/die Jude / Jüdin (en) (nen)
Moslem	der/die Moslem (en) (nen)
Quaker	der/die Quaker/in (-) (nen)
Jehovah's witness	die Zeugen Jehovas
God	Gott
the Buddha	Buddha
Christ	Christus
Mohammed	Mohammed
the prophet	der Prophet (en)
Allah	Allah
cathedral	die Kathedrale (n)
chapel	die Kapelle (n)
church	die Kirche (n)
mosque	die Moschee (n)
temple	der Tempel (-)
synagogue	die Synagoge (n)
religious leader	das Religionsoberhaupt ("er)
bishop	der Bischof ("e)
pope	der Papst
Dalai Lama	der Dalai Lama
imam	der Imam (s)
monk	der Mönch (e)
nun	die Nonne (n)
priest	der Priester (-)
rabbi	der Rabbi (s)
prayer	das Gebet (e)
mass	die Messe (n)
baptism	die Taufe (n)

christening	die Taufe (n)
to take refuge	Zuflucht nehmen
communion	die Kommunion (en)
wedding	die Hochzeit (en)
funeral	die Beerdigung (en)
religious	religiös
religion	die Religion (en)
affiliation	die Zugehörigkeit
religious affiliation	die Religionszugehörigkeit
religiousness	die Religiösität
religious community	die Religionsgemeinschaft

Social issues

community	die Gemeinschaft
charities	die Wohlfahrtsverbände
social services	die Sozialdienste
social work	die Sozialarbeit
fundamental problems	fundamentale Probleme
financial problems	finanzielle Probleme
poverty	die Armut
debt	die Schulden
psychological problems	die psychologischen Probleme
depression	die Depression (en)
emotional deprivation	die emotionale Deprivation
drug problems	die Drogenprobleme
alcohol problems	die Alkoholprobleme
insecurity	die Unsicherheit (en)
loneliness	die Einsamkeit
mental health	die geistige Gesundheit
neglect	vernachlässigen
racial tension	die rassistischen Spannungen
stress	der Stress
unemployment	die Arbeitslosigkeit
homelessness	die Obdachlosigkeit
environmental problems	die Umweltprobleme
bad housing	die schlechten Wohnverhältnisse
family problems	die Familienprobleme
lack of food/water	die Lebensmittelknappheit/ Wasserknappheit
overcrowding	die Überbevölkerung
poverty	die Armut

unhealthy living conditions	ungesunde Lebensbedingungen
bad environment	das schlechte Umfeld
help/ assistance	die Hilfe
social worker	der/die Sozialarbeiter/in (-) (nen)

Useful verbs

to attend church	zur Kirche gehen
to believe	glauben
to pray	beten
to preach	predigen
to kneel	knien
to sing, chant	singen
to worship	anbeten
to meditate	meditieren
to do charity work	freiwilligen Dienst in sozialen Einrichtungen machen
to counsel	beraten
to assist	helfen

More vocabulary

work	die Arbeit
the figures	die Zahlen
unemployment figures	die Arbeitslosenzahlen
creation	die Beschaffung
measure/action	die Maßnahmen
job creation scheme	die Arbeitsbeschaffungs-maßnahmen

16

the media

16.1 The press

Core vocabulary

media	die Medien
press	die Presse
newspaper	die Zeitung (en)
national newspaper	die überregionale Zeitung (en)
magazine	die Zeitschrift (en)/die Illustrierte (en)
review	der Überblick (e)
tabloid paper	die Boulevardzeitung (en)
trash magazines	die Regenbogenpresse
daily	täglich
weekly	wöchentlich
bi-weekly	14-täglich
monthly	monatlich
annual	jährlich
publisher	der/die Verleger/in (-) (nen)
editor	der/die Redakteur/in (-) (nen)/ Herausgeber/in (-) (nen)
journalist	der/die Journalist/in (-) (nen)
journalism	der/die Journalismus
reporter	der/die Reporter/in (-) (nen)
correspondent	der/die Korrespondent/in (-) (nen)
critic	die Kritik (en)
leading article	der Leitartikel (-)
current events	aktuelle Ereignisse (-)
headline	die Schlagzeile (n)
column	die Kolumne (-)
article	der Artikel (-)
advertisement	die Anzeige (n)
notices	die Bekanntmachungen
obituaries	der Nachruf (e), die Todesanzeige(n)
small ads	die Kleinanzeigen/die Inserate
local news	die Lokalnachrichten
news items	die Nachrichten
natural disasters	die Naturkatastrophen
floods	die Überflutungen
drought	die Dürre
famine	die Hungersnot (¨e)
earthquake	das Erdbeben (-)

epidemic	die Seuche (n)
volcano	der Vulkanausbruch (¨e)
storm/hurricane	der Wirbelsturm (¨e)/der Orkan (e)
car crash	der Autounfall (¨e)
plane crash	das Flugzeugunglück (e)
collision at sea	der Schiffzusammenstoß (¨e)
terrorist attack	das terroristische Attentat (-e)
bomb attack	der Bombenanschlag (¨e)
to hijack a plane	ein Flugzeug entführen
taking a hostage	die Geiselnahme (n)
political demonstration	die politische Demonstration (en)
strike	der Streik (s)
fire	das Feuer (-)
forest fire	der Waldbrand (¨e)

Useful verbs

to give one's view on	sich darüber äußern
to complain	beklagen
to remind	mahnen
to enter into negotiations	in Verhandlungen treten
to appoint	beauftragen
to demand	verlangen
to publish	veröffentlichen
explain/to say	erklären
to announce	bekannt geben
to gain	erzielen
to announce	verkünden
to consult	beraten
to announce	<u>an</u>kündigen

i Newspaper reports are written mainly in the imperfect tense:

Alle politischen Parteien trafen sich zu einer Versammlung.
All political parties met for a meeting.

Mehrere Einbrüche wurden in der Innenstadt gemeldet.
Several burglaries were reported in the city centre.

Ein Jugendlicher ertrank in dem Dorfsee.
One youngster drowned in the village lake.

Der Zusammenstoß zweier Autos auf der A5 resultierte in 5 verletzten Personen.
The collision of two cars on the A5 resulted in 5 people being injured.

Different types of paper

Some daily German newspapers

Bild Zeitung; shortened to *Bild*
Westdeutsche Allgemeine Zeitung
Hannoversche Allgemeine Zeitung
Süddeutsche Zeitung
Frankfurter Allgemeine Zeitung
Die Welt
Berliner Morgenpost
Der Tagesspiegel

Some weekly and Sunday newspapers

Bild am Sonntag
Die Zeit
Welt am Sonntag
Bayernkurier

Some news magazines

Der Spiegel
Der Stern
Focus

Periodicals

Die Bunte
Brigitte
Cosmopolitan
Freundin

16.2 Books

Core vocabulary

title	der Titel (-)
author	der/die Schriftsteller/in (-) (nen)
artist	der/die Künstler/in (-) (nen)
illustrator	der/die Illustrator/in (-) (nen)
cartoonist	der/die Cartoonist/in (-) (nen)
biography	die Biografie (n)
autobiography	die Autobiografie (n)
novel	der Roman (e)
romantic novel	der Liebesroman (e)
poetry	die Poesie (-)
short story	die Kurzgeschichte (n)
narrative	die Erzählung (en)
paperback	das Taschenbuch (¨er)
dictionary	das Wörterbuch (¨er)
encyclopedia	das Lexikon (Lexika)
atlas	der Atlas (Atlanten)

guide book	das Sachbuch (¨er)
light fiction	die Unterhaltungsliteratur
literature for women	die Frauenliteratur
literature for children	die Kinderliteratur
punctuation	die Zeichensetzung (en)
paragraph	der Absatz (¨e)
sentence	der Satz (¨e)
line	die Zeile (n)
capital letter	der Großbuchstabe (n)
full stop	der Punkt (e)
comma	das Komma (s)
dash	der Gedankenstrich (e)
hyphen	der Bindestrich (e)
upper case	der Großbuchstabe (n)
lower case (letters)	der Kleinbuchstabe (n)

Useful verbs

to write	schreiben	*to describe*	beschreiben
to develop	entwickeln	*to portray*	darstellen/
to publish	veröffent-		schildern
	lichen	*to quote*	zitieren
to write poems	dichten	*to express*	<u>aus</u>drücken

16.3 Cinema and television

Core vocabulary

cinema	das Kino (s)
auditorium	der Zuschauerraum (¨e)
screen	die Leinwand (¨e)
seat	der Platz (¨e)
foyer	die Eingangshalle (n)
ticket	die Kinokarte (n)
booking office	die Kinokasse (n)
popcorn	das Popcorn
film	der Film (e)
thriller	der Krimi(s), der Thriller
romance	der romantische Film
love story	der Liebesfilm
historical film	der Geschichtsfilm
science fiction	der Science-Fictionfilm
horror film	der Horrorfilm
war film	der Kriegsfilm

comedy	die Komödie (n)
crime	der Kriminalfilm (e)
adverts	die Werbung
film star	der Filmstar (s)
actor/actress	der/die Schauspieler/in (-) (nen)
leading role	die Hauptrolle (n)
supporting role	die Nebenrolle (n)
singer	der/die Sänger/in (-) (nen)
dancer	der/die Tänzer/in (-) (nen)
director	der/die Direktor/in (en) (nen)
producer	der/die Produzent/in (en) (nen)
cameraman	der/die Kameramann/ frau (¨er) (en)
the crew	die Filmbesatzung
video	das Video (s)
DVD	DVD
the film is dubbed	der Film ist synchronisiert
subtitled	der Film hat Untertitel
television	das Fernsehen (-)
cable TV	das Kabelfernsehen
satellite	der Satellit (en)
dish	der Satellitenempfänger
aerial	die Antenne (n)
video recorder	der Videoapparat (e)
DVD *recorder*	der DVD-Spieler
remote control	die Fernbedienung (en)
channel	der Kanal (¨e)
commercials (adverts)	die Werbung (en)
cartoons	der Zeichentrickfilm (e)
children's programmes	das Kinderprogramm (e)
chat show	die Talkshow (s)
documentary	die Dokumentation (en)
feature film	der Spielfilm (e)
game show	die Spielshow (s)
light entertainment	leichte Unterhaltung
news programmes	die Nachrichtensendung (en)
opinion	die Meinung (en)
quiz	das Quiz (e)
soap	die Seifenoper (n)
weather forecast	der Wetterbericht (e)
repeats	die Wiederholungen
news reporter	der/die Nachrichten- journalist/in (en) (nen)
news reader	der/die Nachrichtensprecher/in (en) (nen)

presenter	der/die Moderator/in (en) (nen)
interviewer	der/die Interviewer/in (en) (nen)
commentator	der/die Kommentator/in (en) (nen)
game show host	der/die Gastgeber/in (en) (nen) der Spielshow
viewer	der/die Zuschauer/in (-) (nen)
radio	das Radio (s)
programme	das Programm (e)
frequency	die Frequenz (en)
disc jockey	der Discjockey (s)

Useful phrases

What is your favourite programme?	Was ist Ihr/dein Lieblingsprogramm?
Do you like documentaries?	Mögen Sie/magst du Dokumentarsendungen?
Who is your favourite presenter?	Wer ist Ihr(e)/dein(e) Lieblingsmoderator/in?

Useful verbs

to change channels	auf einen anderen Sender <u>um</u>schalten
to turn on/off the telly	das Fernsehen <u>ein</u>schalten/<u>aus</u>schalten
to turn the sound up/down	die Lautstärke <u>auf</u>drehen/<u>runter</u>drehen
to broadcast	berichten
to record	<u>auf</u>nehmen, <u>auf</u>zeichnen

ℹ Drei deutsche Regisseure der heutigen Zeit und ihre Filme (three current German film directors and their films)

Doris Dörrie
• *Nackt* (2002) (*Naked*) • *Erleuchtung garantiert* (2000) (*Enlightment Guaranteed*) • *Bin ich schön?* (1998) *Am I beautiful?*
Rainer Werner Fassbinder
• *Fassbinder in Hollywood* (2002) • *Last Trip to Harrisburg* (1984)
• *Sehnsucht der Veronika Voss* (1982) (*Veronika Voss*) • *Lili Marlee* (1981)
Wim Wenders
• *The Blues* (2002) • *Viel passiert* (2002) (*Ode to Cologne*)
• *Ten Minutes Older* (2002) • *Million Dollar Hotel* (2000)